THE BOOK OF LIGHTS · II

UNVEILING
THE MYSTERY OF
CHRIST

Spiritual Translations By

JOHN A. PARRY

P&P
Publishing

The Book of Lights—II
Unveiling the Mystery of Christ
by John A. Parry

Published by:
P & P Publishing
P.O. Box 1051
Warren, Michigan, 48090 U.S.A.

Bible quotes appearing in this presentation were taken from the King James version. For purposes of clarity, the author has occasionally rephrased the wording in order to better convey his Spiritual intent. Phrases in italics are the author's comments.

Edited by Sid Korpi
Typesetting by Lightbourne, Inc.

Preassigned LCCN: 2004090759
ISBN: 0-9745740-1-5

Cover design by **Lightbourne, Inc.,** © 2004.

Cover picture provided by Brad Perks
PC Image Network, © 2004

TABLE OF CONTENTS

Introduction

U nveiling the Mystery of Christ is the second presentation
of a three-book series entitled *The Book of Lights.*
Whereas the tenets in *Unveiling the Mystery of God,* the
first book in the series, centered on recognizing the historical pattern that mankind was to follow in his quest for life eternal, this
current presentation builds upon that historical foundation by
further expanding the mind's view of what constitutes Christ's
return in the Father's eternal glory and the Father's promise to
make "the kingdom of heaven" available to all mankind. Because
that promise was Spiritually fulfilled, dating back some two thousand years, this presentation specifically identifies "the kingdom
of God," or "the kingdom of heaven," as an ever-present Spiritual
state; an eternal reality that is immediately available to those who
seek entry into its everlasting glory.

You will discover in studying this segment of *The Book of
Lights* that the mind's passage from mortality to immortality is
viewed as free of time-related restrictions. It contends that eternal enlightenment is readily accomplished through the Spiritual
translation of countless Word similes — as opposed to the pop-
ular belief that mankind's passage into an immortal state lies
beyond the grave. Consequently, converting the Word's instructional imagery into the unifying truths that God intended to
convey is critical to the reader's Spiritual ascent; for until the

Creator's image and likeness is transposed into related forms of comprehension, the mind cannot attain the glory it seeks. Accordingly, we see Christ identifying himself, *and by extension all mankind*, with the Word's correlative similes, resolutely declaring, "No man comes to the Father except by me," *except by Spiritually translating the Word's unifying imagery and recognizing the relationship he shares with God through those similes.*

Since this progressive series is structured as a study in Spiritual self-discovery, the reader should be eminently aware that *Unveiling the Mystery of Christ* is not about religious worship, nor is it about morals or social history. It is about you, the reader. If the reader initially fails to relate to the various dimensions of truth that appear in this presentation, he should not be discouraged. Beginning at birth, all life emerges from darkness and ascends into the light. True Spirituality is no different. It is interwoven into mankind's Life experience. We must therefore labor to understand our unity with God, for the glory we seek is attained through those labors.

To unite in Spirit and in truth with this everlasting state, the timeline that impedes all Spiritual thought must be removed. We must look beyond the linear illusion of times and places; and beyond the appearance of names and faces. We must see our face in all faces, to understand that we are a composite of the continuous whole. The first step toward life eternal will then be taken, and the reader will begin to know himself, even as he is known in the eyes of The Eternal.

By relating to the truths set forth in this presentation, the reader's understanding of himself, and the Spiritual world that God has so diligently labored to prepare for mankind, should be greatly enhanced. Entry into this world of "the Most High" should lead to the reader's success in turning back the flood of misconceptions that religious doctrines presently impose upon God's labors. As Christ said, "It is my Father's good pleasure to give you his kingdom." It should be our pleasure to graciously accept and to understand what God has made ready for us.

Because eternal truth is supportive of its own kind and never stands alone, you will find *Unveiling the Mystery of God* and *Unveiling the Mystery of Christ* invaluable in clarifying each other. Reflective of this unifying characteristic, when the reader adopts the truths set forth in these two presentations, his sealed image and likeness in God is quickened. The law of Life is Spiritually fulfilled, and mankind's eternal character is revealed. All things thereafter coalesce into one all-inclusive body, and God becomes all in all.

*I have come as a light into the world
that you should not abide in darkness.*

SPIRITUAL TRANSLATIONS

*Whosoever will let him take freely of
the waters of Life.*

1

A New Spiritual Orientation

"If there should be a messenger, an interpreter, one among a thousand who will show man his uprightness, I will say, Deliver him from going down into the pit. I have found a ransom."

JOB 33:23-24

For some six thousand years, people of all religious persuasions have labored to understand the complex mystery of man's Spiritual heritage. Their efforts have met only with limited success. Why? Because the mystery of man cannot be resolved until the mystery of God and his Christ is settled. Since the enigma of their interwoven relationship continues to elude the body's sensory faculties, all that is eternally true goes unrecognized and man's Spiritual aspirations remain unfulfilled.

To understand our eternal heritage in Christ, we must return to that timeless Age when the Creator caused his light to shine out of darkness; for when God said, "Let there be light," *as set forth in the Genesis analogy,* a variance in potential occurred within the void. A Life-emitting flow of energy was set in motion, and the light emitted by that flow was made to shine out of darkness. Therein, "two witnesses" were formed; one of Life and one of light. As energy shared in common, the Life was embodied in the light, and the light was embodied in the Life. The light of Life thereafter appeared as the founding tenet of a boundless Universe. As Christ confirmed, "Two witnesses fulfill the law of Life." ("The Father witnesses and I witness also.")

Since the Bible identifies Creation's first light as the Christ, *the light within the Life,* and recognizes that characterization as "the true light that lights every man coming into the world," it follows that Life's all-inclusive light cannot be limited to a particular person. Rather, it supports the truth that at mankind's inception, when the light of Life ("the breath of Life") was imparted to man, he became an eternal parallelism. We must therefore conclude that, by design, man has direct access to God's eternal Spirit. Embracing this "God made man" evidence, Jesus personified the light's presence, declaring, "I am the Way, the Truth, and the Life. I am in the Father, *the Creator,* and the Father is in me. He that has seen me has seen the Father, *has seen the Creator.*"

To enhance our understanding of Christ's role in characterizing the light of Life, it would be beneficial to review the time sequence that presaged the birth of Jesus of Nazareth; for in him Creation's "first light" was transposed into mankind's "true light" for all to see.

In the beginning, when the Spirit of God emerged from the dark abyss, the light, *identified by Scripture as the Word-body of Christ,* emerged with him. Billions of years would pass, however, before Life's quickened light would appear in human form. ("I am the light of the world.") This initial transposing of primordial elements into visible manifestation was, nevertheless, the forerunner of a quickening process that continues to this day. Thereafter, the light of Life would appear within all living things and culminate in the revelatory body of Jesus Christ. ("In him all things have their consistency.")

John's Gospel speaks of the universal presence of God and Christ within natural form when he writes, "He was in the world, and the world was made by him, but the world knew him not." The apostle Paul also refers to the Creator's unifying light when he chides his followers, "Though we deny him, yet he abides faithful. He cannot deny himself."

In contrast to the limitations of will-worship presently imposed by the religious community upon the Son of man, consider the Bible's various expressions of Christ's all-inclusive attendance:

- He is the "Tree of Life," *the light of Life,* that resides in the midst of the Garden of God.
- He is the revelatory light that appeared in the Creator's historical signs and wonders, the similes conveyed to mankind for Spiritual instruction.
- He is the "Word of the law," the witnessing light that God imparted to Moses to show mankind the regenerative principles upon which the creative process was founded.
- He is the "Promised Land" that was covenanted to mankind for an everlasting heritage.
- He is the "Son of man" who was quickened and appeared within all the prophets.
- He is the "Word made flesh" that appeared in bodily form as Jesus Christ.
- He is "the Holy Ghost" that resides in God, the Spirit of truth that leads mankind through heaven's gate.

To distinguish between the Creator and the manifesting light-patterns that comprise his work, this presentation portrays God as Spirit and Life — a quickening entity who alone is "Spiritual." In contrast, because the light within his Spirit is out-pictured into elemental form, all created manifestation is portrayed as pseudo-spiritual. Notwithstanding, in the end time when the reconciling process is finished ("It is finished.") and the pseudo-spiritual Christ ascends to the Father, all is united and transposed into the "Spiritual" Paradise of God. All pseudo-spiritual life is then raised *without error,* and God becomes all in all. ("I am the resurrection and the Life.") *I am the light that provides mankind with resurrection, and I am* the Life *that provides the light.*

Upon discovering that God's Spiritual character was conveyed to mankind through natural manifestation, seekers of eternal truth perceived the earth and all the stars of heaven as a living symbolic language, a transposing of principles acting in concert with the Creator's Spirit. That discovery was emphasized when the light emanating from Sinai's bush instructed Moses, "Tell the children of Israel that I AM has sent you, *I AM the light of Life within Creation.* I AM that I AM."

One of the few books of Scripture depicting the glory God had bestowed upon his witnessing light is found in the book of Proverbs. That characterization reads:

"The Lord possessed me in the beginning of his ways, before his works of old.

I was set up from everlasting; from the beginning or ever the earth was formed.

When there were no depths, I was brought forth; when there were no fountains abounding with water, before the mountains were settled, or before the hills appeared, I was brought forth.

When he prepared the heavens, I was there; when he set a compass upon the face of the deep, I was with him.

Then was I by him, as one brought up with him; and I was daily his delight, rejoicing always before him.

Blessed is the man that hears me; for he that finds me finds Life. And he shall find favor with the Lord."

Since God's revelatory light is so deeply and intricately woven into his labors, we should expect the principles which inherently support that relationship to provide the keys so necessary to understanding man's place in the Creator's progressive work. In that regard, we are not disappointed. Correlating the principles that appear in natural manifestation provides us with two of those keys.

The first principle appears in the law of "Cause and Effect," the law that everything is to reproduce after its own kind. In reference to this present discussion, Cause represents the Creator and Effect represents Creation.

The second principle relates to uniformity. It states, "Things equal to the same thing are equal to each other;" that whatsoever God or man plants they shall also reap.

Because all of God's work achieves unity through the correlation of these two principles, we find the second law working in conjunction with the first. When viewed individually, these two laws appear to differ. Nevertheless, they are parallelisms. Their witness is interwoven.

Since Creation visibly expresses the invisible character of its Source, the visible and the invisible must be viewed as equal to each other. ("As above, so below.")

Fully aware that all manifestation had these two witnesses within itself, Jesus explained, "All that the Father has are mine, and all mine are the Father's." Because the witness of Moses and the prophets was an extension of Creation's originating principle, Christ assured the Jews, "Not one comma or period shall be removed from God's witnessing light." Nothing can change its quickening power. The Creator's "true and faithful witness" is thus recognized as residing in the light-patterns wherein all manifestation originates; however, this principle would not be recognized by mankind until that age when the Son of man emerged within the prophets, *and afterwards, in the Word-body of Christ.*

With the visible light-patterns that characterized God's invisible Spirit in the above now reappearing as pseudo-spiritual manifestation in the below, the authors of Scripture compared Creation's inherent light-patterns to angels of the Most High, *a heavenly host that Scripture later identified as "the mind of Christ."* In that context, the Son of man spoke of coming to mankind in his Father's glory, bringing all the holy angels, a*ll the light-patterns of God,* with him. In his appearing, Christ's radiant form is thus seen emanating, *in Spirit and in truth,* from the midst of God's work. ("Let all the angels of God witness to him.") By reviewing this progressive order, we validate Scripture's assertion that the light of Life that characterized God's Spirit at Creation's inception was made flesh, giving birth to the tenet of Christ's presence in man. ("No man has seen the Father at any time. The only begotten, *the light of Life,* which is in the bosom of the Father, he has declared him.")

Fashioned as an extension of the Creator's character, Christ's radiant form thus appeared in all that God had made. It was his emanating presence to which all of the law and the prophets witnessed. When Isaiah recognized his attendance as an intangible light dwelling in the midst of tangible form, he wrote, "When we shall see him, he has neither form nor comeliness that we should desire him." Christ's character is thus recognized as a formal correlation of God's presence within his unfolding work.

In studying Scripture, we discover that the word "Creation," which refers to both visible and invisible form, and "Christ," which refers to the light embodied within both visible and invisible form, are terms equal to each other. This is verified in the following:

- "The only begotten, which is in the bosom of the Father, *the Christ which is in the bosom of Creation,* he has declared him."
- "The same, *Christ, or light within Creation,* was in the beginning with God."
- "Who being the brightness of the Father's glory and the express image of his person, *a parallelism,* when he had by himself purged our errors sat down at the right hand of the majesty on high."
- "He, *the Christ, or light within Creation,* is the image of the invisible God, the firstborn of every creature."
- "He, *the Christ, or light within Creation,* was in the world and the world was made by him, but the world knew him not."
- "Of myself, *the Christ, or light within Creation,* I can do nothing. It is the Father, *the Life,* within me that does the work."
- "I, *the Christ, or light within Creation,* am the Way, the Truth, and the Life, *an incarnation of the Life that emerged from the dark abyss.* No man comes to the Father except by me."

By making these comparisons we confirm that Christ, *or the light within Creation,* appeared as a correlation of the energizing principle that emerged from the dark abyss as the light of Life. Still, billions of years would pass before this principle was recognized and identified as the presence of the living God.

Notwithstanding, God's manifesting work would need refinement. After Creation's primordial phase was in place, a defect was discovered, a weakness that required a reconciling of the Creator's labors. ("My Father works hitherto and I work also.") In causing his light to shine out of darkness, God had not only given Life to his inherent light but had also given Life to the darkness within the primal void. Responding to the reproductive law, voidal darkness had brought forth after its own kind and now mingled with the Creator's inherent principles, and that incursion created a temporal abstraction: an anomaly expressed as Eden's Tree of Knowledge of good and evil.

To reconcile this intrusive phenomenon, God formed man from the dust of the ground, creating a pseudo-spiritual inversion of his light. ("Let us make man in our image and after our likeness.") Formed as a microcosm of all things preceding him, the first man, Adam, emerged as Creation's living voice: God's living Word. The task of reconciling the darkness that appeared within the Creator's work thus came to rest on Adam, and upon the Christ whose light now latently resided within Adam's mind and body. ("The secret kept from the foundation of the world: Christ in us, the hope of glory.")

Scripture hastens to assure us that without regard to the deception experienced by the first couple in Eden, mankind was not inherently evil. ("Now lest the man put forth his hand and eat of the Tree of Life, *the light of Life,* and live forever.") Accordingly, man's sensory body was fashioned to transpose Creation's visible elements into invisible thought-patterns, and his mind was fashioned to characterize the angels of light, *the enlightening patterns of Truth,* that witnessed from the midst of visible manifestation.

As a replica of all things pertaining to the Most High, Adam's Spiritual side was equivalent to the Holy of Holies that was fashioned by Moses at Sinai. In relating man to this instructive analogy, Moses envisioned the Ark of God as being shouldered by four men, depicting the four levels of comprehension available to mankind, *two levels mirroring the pseudo-spiritual mind and two levels mirroring the Spiritual mind.* The three Oracles housed within the Ark represented the latent true light which resided within man's pseudo-spiritual knowledge and the two Archangels, which faced each other on the covering of the Ark, signified the two witnesses that forever tied the Life in the above to the light in the below. As a pseudo-spiritual expression of all that the Father of lights had made, temporal-minded Adam had emerged with Christ as two entities evolving in one body. ("A body *of reconciliation* you have prepared for me.") Therein, Christ assumed his place in the wilderness of mankind's confused and darkened cognizance.

With God's radiant glory now latently embodied in man, Christ's all-inclusive light was referred to as "He that has the seven spirits of God," or the sum of the seven-day analogy of Creation. Those Spiritual elements are identified in man as follows:

The elemental aspects of the four spirits of the heavens are recognized in man as Fire, Water, Earth and Air. The principles relating to those four divisions are in accord with God's Spirit and are viewed as extensions of his person.

The remaining three spirits of the heavens appear as mankind's three progressive levels of comprehension: his temporal reality, his pseudo-spiritual reality, and his Spiritual reality.

These seven spirits are witnessed in all of the Creator's work and ultimately surface within Scripture's revelation as Christ's all-inclusive inheritance. ("He that holds the seven stars in his right hand and walks among the seven golden candlesticks.") The prophets referred to these seven entities as "the seven spirits of God that run to and fro throughout the whole earth."

Since the elements that fashioned Adam were an extension of Christ's pseudo-spiritual glory, it followed that the outer darkness that afflicted mankind also afflicted Christ. Therefore, as one, Christ and man began their interwoven sojourn on earth estranged from comprehending the principles of God. Reverting to their primordial heritage, all was cloaked in outer darkness. All witnessed to the temporal state that emerged with God from the primordial abyss. ("He made darkness his pavilion and dark clouds his secret place.")

With those primal limitations now in evidence, the Creator's work was split into three levels of judgment. Those three levels are detailed throughout Scripture and are identified within man as follows:

- On the first level of judgment, primal darkness emerged from the void and brought forth after its own kind; endowing the psyche with a reality that was of the earth, earthy. That reality appeared as the temporal mind and was expressed by Genesis as "Cain," a tiller of the soil, *the firstborn of mankind.*

- On the second level of judgment, God's Spirit, having emerged from the primal void, was clothed upon with formal light. ("The light of Life.") However, because his light witnessed to both light and darkness, *knowledge of good and evil,* it too succumbed to darkness. That reality appeared in man as the pseudo-spiritual mind, expressed by Genesis as "Abel," a keeper of flocks, *the second-born of mankind,* whom Cain slew.

- On the third level of judgment, God's true light emerged from the void and was clothed upon in its all-encompassing glory. Therein, all was judged in Spirit and in truth. That reality appeared in man as the Spiritual mind, *"The mind of Christ,"* expressed by Genesis as "Seth," *the third-born of mankind,* in whom God's eternal seed was made manifest.

We should be aware, however, that in Creation's primordial phase, these three levels of reality had yet to be interpreted. All continued to evolve, mirroring the Creator's experience when he emerged from the primal abyss. The darkness that was native to his Spirit thus moved upon on the face of the deep. It would not be until Moses wrote the simile of Adam and Eve exiting Eden that these three levels of comprehension would be identified and God's labor of reconciling the darkness that intruded into God's work would begin.

2

The Integrating of Christ and Man

"This is the mystery kept throughout the Ages. The mystery that is now made manifest to all generations: Christ in us, the hope of glory."

COLOSSIANS 1:26,27

In beginning this segment on *Unveiling the Mystery of Christ*, two important factors must be considered. First, God's Spirit within Creation, *and within man*, is multidimensional. Second, upon imparting Christ's light to Adam, as integrated entities, they two became the Creator's chosen vehicle for reconciling the diverse aspects of his work. ("Let us make man in our image and after our likeness.") Fashioned as an expression of God's character in microcosm, Christ and man thus began to evolve as two in one body, as one all-inclusive entity. Therein, they progressed in concert with the inherent principles upon which all of the Creator's work was based. ("Whatsoever the Father does the Son does likewise.") In that relationship, they two assumed the semblance of Creation's voice, God's living Word, and as joint heirs of everything preceding their union, they were afflicted by the dark anomaly that emerged from the abyss and intruded into the Creator's work. ("In all our afflictions, he was afflicted.")

Mirroring the relationship that existed between Creation's manifesting light and its quickening Source, Adam's mind and body personalized their semblance in microcosm. In this reconfiguring of attributes, his mind was equivalent to the Creator's life-quickening ability ("I am the Life.") and his body was equal to the elemental light-forms that comprised Creation. ("I am the light of Life.") As two in one body, Christ and man thus inherited the role of reconciling all the works of God, and all began with the Spirit of God moving upon the face of the deep.

To overcome the dark anomaly that encroached upon his labors, and to give Christ's invisible presence in man recognition, the Creator now embarked upon a course of creating correlative signs and wonders, similes that mirrored the principles upon which his work was founded. Commencing with the departure of Adam and Eve from Eden, he began flooding the earth with enlightening parallelisms, similitudes that conveyed the reciprocal principles imparted to Christ and man at their union. Therein, a foundation was laid to reconcile the Creator's work and to exit from darkness into light. ("I have come as a light into the world that you should not abide in darkness.") Historically, this reconciling effort began with Abraham's calling and culminated with Christ's agonizing cry at Golgotha, "It is finished!" ("Father, I have finished the work you gave me to do.")

Thus, as two in one body, the latent Christ in concert with temporal-minded man entered into a regenerative Age. Empowered by the Creator, they began to reconcile the fragmented appearance within his work, bringing to light the eternal principles that emanated from within his Spirit. Therein, the kingdom of heaven was identified and its glory was made known. ("You shall see Abraham, Isaac, and Jacob, and all the prophets set down in the kingdom of heaven.") As the transposing of the Creator's instructional signs and wonders increased,

Christ and man became progressively cognizant of God's glory, and their pseudo-spiritual unity was recognized as having a three-dimensional nature.

- The first level of their combined union was temporal and witnessed to their inherent earthy nature. ("The first man is of the earth, earthy.")
- The second level of their combined union was pseudo-spiritual and witnessed to a mixing of temporal and pseudo-spiritual elements. ("If the light in you be darkness, then your darkness is great.")
- The third level of their combined union was Spiritual and witnessed to the inherent unity that joined God, Christ and Man together as one all-inclusive entity. This level of comprehension was initially latent, however, and would not be recognized or experienced until the Son of man's inborn presence was revealed and Spiritual maturity was imparted to the psyche. ("In the third day, he shall raise us up.")

The stage was thus set for further reconciliation, and the Father of lights began dividing his light from the outer darkness that intruded into his work.

Since the Creator's purpose in flooding the earth with signs and wonders was to unify all things within himself, when Jesus came preaching salvation to the Jews he immediately related his message to God's revelatory work. Correlating his analogies to indicate their relationship to the Creator's outpictured similes, he explained, "No man comes to the Father except by me; and no man comes to me except the Father, who has sent me, draw him." That is, *No man comes to the principles that comprise the Father's person except by his light, and no man comes to the principles embodied in his light except the witnessing signs and wonders that the Father has sent draw him.* Concurring with this sealed relationship, we read: "The only begotten who is in the bosom of the Father, he has declared him." The earth was thus flooded with instructional similes in an effort to focus man on achieving true judgment, for without true judgment, there could be no Spiritual reconciliation.

On the other hand, because the thoughts of all generations were swayed by the void's intrusive darkness, the temporal mind continued to give life to an anomaly that worked against God's effort to reconcile his work. Consequently, the Creator's signs and wonders were constantly made of non-effect. ("All we like sheep have gone astray. We have turned, every one, to his own way and the Lord has laid upon him, *upon Christ's true light within man,* the inequity of us all.") Countless generations would pass before a select few would be Spiritually awakened to the truth that the Creator's witnessing light was imparted to man but was journeying with him in an unrecognized state. In reaching that level of understanding, their thoughts would be raised from a pseudo-spiritual to a Spiritual level of comprehension and begin witnessing to The Eternal. ("Except the Lord had left us a remnant we would have been as Sodom and like unto Gomorrah.")

With the mind's awakening to its eternal heritage, the prophet Elijah, as the forerunner of Israel's prophets, was translated into heaven. With his reappearing as the Son of man within the prophets, the signs and wonders that provided the foundation for his ascent were Spiritually transposed. ("If you see me when I am taken up, a double portion of my spirit, *the Word's external and internal witness,* shall be upon you.") In the course of that event, Elijah's servant, Elisha, saw his master's translation and recognized it as a quickening of mirrored similes. Ecstatic over this flash of enlightenment, he exclaimed, "My Father! My Father! You are the Chariot of Israel, *the light of Spiritual instruction conveyed to Israel,* and the horsemen, *the Spiritual truths,* thereof!"

With that recognition, Elijah's mantle, the *external covering that concealed Christ's presence,* fell from him and Elisha, *seeing the Son of man's internal presence,* picked up the mantle. The secret that led to Elijah's translation was thus made known to all the prophets. ("He reveals his secret, *the power of translation,* to his servants the prophets.") Thereafter, all the prophets followed Elijah's lead. They transposed the Creator's instructional signs and wonders into themselves and testified to the threefold manifestation that appeared throughout his regenerative work.

Using the desolations of Israel and the ensuing tribulation that attended those times, they likened the light of Life within man to "the voice of one crying in the wilderness." Their mission thus became one of furthering God's work of reconciliation, of revealing the Son of man's presence within their midst, and preparing a highway in the desert for the light that was witnessed in all that God had made.

The overwhelming importance of the Age of the prophets is that these Way-showers of God had attained the ability to Spiritually translate his enlightening similes, and his effort to dispel the darkness that impeded his work had finally born fruit. Mankind had not only obtained external and internal verification of the Creator's presence, it also obtained living proof that all generations had direct access to his eternal Spirit. This externalizing of the Creator's signs and wonders came to an abrupt end when Jesus informed the Jews, "The law and the prophets, *the external witness of God's signs and wonders,* were until John. Now, the kingdom of God, *the internal witness of his signs and wonders,* is preached."

So, with the culminating of Christ's portrayal of God's Word in man, *his portrayal of the light of Life in man,* and his death at Golgotha, the Creator's outpictured instruction ceased. All that outwardly appeared divided was now inwardly reconciled. As one all-inclusive body, the Christ who resided within man delivered up those who, *through Spiritual translation,* achieved unity with his Spirit. The continuous whole of God's work thus ascended with Christ and became eternally One with the Father in heavenly places. ("I came out from the Father, now I return to the Father.")

Thereafter, the eternal union that Christ and Man had achieved with the Creator reappeared in Spirit and in truth, leading mankind into all truth. ("A little while and the world shall see me no more; but you shall see me, and because I live you shall live also.")

3

The Perfecting of Christ and Man

"Be therefore perfect, even as your Father in heaven is perfect."

MATTHEW 5:48

There was perhaps no time more crucial in man's history than the Age of the prophets, for those days marked the passing of God's glory in external signs and wonders into a new Age; a time when the Creator would appear within man's consciousness and reveal his inherent true light as an eternal entity. ("And this is life eternal, to know God and Jesus Christ whom he has sent.")

However, the ascent and perfecting of Christ and Man with God's glory hinged upon the mind's ability to unite with Christ and to become one with all that the Father of lights had made. Individually, or collectively, his generations would need to look inward and behold the light of Life that had issued from the foundation of the world and begin reconciling their thoughts to its radiant presence. ("This is the true light that lights every man coming into the world.") The glory that God had imparted to Christ through created form would then be Spiritually quickened, reappearing within man as the Collective Consciousness of

God's eternal kingdom. ("He has translated us into the kingdom of his beloved Son.")

Jesus compared this climatic transformation of the psyche, *from a pseudo-spiritual to a Spiritual reality,* to the temporal devastation experienced by Israel at the fall of Jerusalem. Using that historic event to depict the tumult that would accompany the psyche's rebirth, he said, "Then shall be great tribulation, such as was not from the beginning of the world to this present time or shall ever be; and except those days should be shortened there should no flesh be saved." Through correlated symbolism, he likened the nullifying of God's first covenant with Israel, and the subsequent fall of their nation to the Gentiles, to the tumult the mind would experience in its departure from traditional will-worship. Therein, he provided a simile wherein all generations could recognize their personal culpability. ("Behold, your house is left unto you desolate; and you shall not see me again until you say, Blessed is he that comes in the name of the Lord.")

The prophets likewise used this historic event as a base for their prophecies. They integrated Israel's catastrophic loss into their work and compared their captivity to the bondage that afflicted Christ. As Isaiah wrote, "In all of their afflictions he was afflicted and the angel of his presence, *the truth that witnessed to his presence,* saved them." These Spiritual Way-showers of God also compared Christ's forthcoming release from bondage to Israel's promised salvation. And, they indicated the price the nations of the earth would pay for obtaining the mind of Christ; a sum that was nonnegotiable. It demanded an end to the mind's pseudo-spiritual warring and its ever-mounting opposition to the inherent principles of God. As the prophet Jeremiah phrased it, "For as long as the land lay desolate she kept Sabbath." Because the Son of man was in the human frame as God's true light, the same price would be required of Christ and man before their deliverance, glorification, and ascent could be achieved. The path that led to life eternal was thus made painfully clear. It decreed that only by bringing an end to the flagrant abuse of God's revelatory instruction could man overcome the power of temporal death. The accumulated error that held his revelatory work in bondage had to end. With removal of the void's dark incursions, only Christ's true light would then remain. *When the "pseudo" aspect of the mind was removed from mankind's pseudo-spiritual nature, only the Spiritual would remain.*

To eliminate any confusion over what divides the mind of the Son of man from the mind of pseudo-spiritual man, we should understand that temporal thought is sensory and based upon reasonable judgments. On the other hand, Spiritual thought is based upon Causal principles and is imparted to the Son of man by God. ("The first man is of the earth, earthy. The second man is the Lord from heaven. As in Adam, all men die, *through error;* so in Christ, all are made alive, *through truth.*")

Since man is a work in progress, all of humanity is required to pass through the mind's three levels of consciousness before ascending to the Father. All therefore embark upon life's journey in darkness, and thereafter progressively ascend into the Ultimate Reality that resides in Christ's light. The Book of Revelation refers to this progressive experience and the subsequent need for crucifying the temporal self, when Christ relates, "I am he that was dead and is alive forevermore. As I overcame and am set down with my Father in his throne, *in the glory of my Father's eternal knowledge,* so to him that overcomes *the mind's first two levels of thought* shall I grant to sit with me in my throne, *in the glory of my eternal knowledge.*"

Until all of God's work is recognized as a projection of enlightening principles, the kingdom of heaven will elude mankind. ("Judge not according to the appearance but judge right judgment.") The truth that God's radiant light within Creation is present within Christ and man is verified in the following:

- "All that the Father has are mine; and all that is mine belongs to the Father." They two are of one image and likeness.
- "The Father and I are one. He that has seen me has seen the Father." They two are of one image and likeness.
- "If the Father is glorified in the Son, he shall glorify the Son within himself." The glory of the two is of one image and likeness.
- "The true light, *the Christ,* within man was made flesh; and we beheld his glory as the only begotten of the Father." The glory shared by God, Christ and Man is of one image and likeness.
- "I came out from the Father, now I return to the Father." The glory of the above is formally replicated in Christ's appearance in the below. They two are of one image and likeness.
- "The Father loves the Son and reveals his Way, his Truth, and his Life to him." The Father loves the Son and has characterized him in his own image and likeness.
- "As above, so below." All in the below is a reflection of heaven's glory. Heaven and earth are full of their image and likeness.
- "Father, all that you have given me I have given to them; that they may be one, even as we are one."

Without recourse, the exiling of the pseudo-spiritual mind from its eternal heritage will continue until all Creation is recognized as an outpicturing of God's Spiritual character. ("All that is under heaven is mine, said the Lord.") By clinging to the errors of preceding generations, humanity shall continue to search for God's truth but shall not find it. However, on the day they depart from the traditional errors of their predecessors and embrace God's revelatory instruction, they shall begin to heal and receive their true inheritance. ("Straight is the gate and narrow is the way that leads to Life, and few there be that find it. But broad is the gate that leads to destruction and many there be that go that way.")

Having provided this Spiritual orientation, and having explained the illuminating glory that God has prepared for Christ and man within his work, the mind's error in what constitutes life eternal should be self-evident. Nonetheless, if the average person were asked to give a comprehensive explanation of God's image and likeness within themselves, much less within the Universe, few would be able to give a satisfactory reply. To most of humanity, God is an enigma, an irresolvable mystery. Yet the majority believes they will one day inherit everlasting life, which is, as Christ explained, "to know God." In view of this conflict in perception, we find ourselves in the same strait as Scripture's famed king of Babylon, when the handwriting appeared on the wall and judged him saying, "You are weighed in the balance and found wanting." For if we are presently unable to relate to the true light that abides within our mortal frame, how can we honestly say that we know God and have life eternal? We cannot! He that relates to the principles of God within himself has life eternal, but he that is without such knowledge has no Life in him. ("Seek first the kingdom of God and his righteousness, and all these things shall be added to you.")

Having weighed the concepts set forth on these pages, it should be clear to all why knowing God is essential to obtaining an eternal heritage. The apostle Paul warned of the mind's temporal limitations when he wrote, "All have erred in temporal judgment and have fallen short of the glory of God." It is time we moved beyond the mind's compulsive errors and experience the realities of truth and perfection. And this we can do by knowing Life as it was, as it is, and as it shall always be; by understanding that all states, though appearing transitory, are eternal.

Throughout the Ages, all generations have struggled and railed against Creation's darkness, all the while not recognizing what they struggled against was rooted in their own character. They have never understood that the mind's inherent darkness was the same as that experienced by God while in his primordial state. ("He that overcomes shall inherit all things.") From generation to generation, we are confronted with the question, "Why does God allow the destructive forces within the world to continue?" The answer of course is their influences exist within us as an extension of the Creator's primordial character. Everlasting life and everlasting shame and contempt will be with us forever, as will our ability to choose whom we shall serve. ("Choose Life for yourself that you might live.") In making this higher choice, we come to an enlightened understanding of our eternal heritage. God's light again shines out of darkness, and we begin to know ourselves even as we are known.

4

The Faces of Man

"For God sent not his Son into the world to condemn the world; but that the world through him might be saved.

He that comes to the Son is not condemned; but he that comes not to him is condemned already, for he has refused the knowledge that God has imparted to the Son.

And this is the condemnation: that light has come into the world, and men loved darkness more than light."

JOHN 3:17-19

There is no truth more explicit than this: No man can know God or comprehend life eternal until he has ceased from believing in a heaven that belongs to the grave and the grave's afterlife. Eternal fulfillment comes only by actively seeking accord with the true light that lies dormant within the human frame. Since the treasures of God are inherently cloaked in darkness, overcoming that anomaly is a prerequisite to obtaining Spiritual light. ("Darkness shall cover the earth and gross darkness the people, but on Christ has the light shined.")

When the Creator extended the radiant light embodied within his work to Adam, the Spiritual light that lay hidden within Creation reappeared in man. As Paul disclosed, this was the secret kept from the foundation of the world: "Christ in us, *God's enlightening principles in us,* the hope of glory." Having arrived at that level of understanding, he cautioned his followers, "Let no man glory in men for all things are yours; for you are Christ's and Christ is God's." All Spiritual enlightenment must therefore abide in harmony with the revelatory light that emanates from Creation's midst, for it is that light, in Christ, which gives insight and Life to the human psyche.

At mankind's origin, when Creation, Christ and man were joined, *in microcosm,* as one all-inclusive body, they inherently mirrored the dark aspect of the Creator's character. The conflicting nature of darkness and light that permeated God's work was therefore defined, *in relationship to man,* as a light shining in a dark place. ("Be mindful of the light that shines in a dark place.") In this configuration, the attributes of darkness conveyed their impressions through the body's sensory faculties while the attributes of light worked in concert with the mind's ability to interpret the in-depth aspects of God's work. ("The Spirit of God moved upon the face of the deep.") In judging by sensory appearance, however, man failed to recognize the inner light wherein his eternal heritage lay hidden. Knowledge of his all-inclusive glory was thus held in abeyance until the various aspects of the Creator's work could be Spiritually reconciled. It was not until the Age of the prophets that the light of Life was openly revealed as dwelling within mankind's midst. ("The people that walked in darkness have seen a great light; they that dwell in the land of the shadow of death, upon them has the light shined.")

There is no question that when Adam unwittingly chose the path of judging by appearance, he assumed the nature of Creation's dark aspect and all knowledge of his Spiritual heritage in God was lost. Cut off from the Creator's true light, he proceeded to view God as an entity apart from himself. As time progressed, he again erred, believing that his deliverance from temporal conflict would be ultimately accomplished through entry into an earthy paradise. This was historically illustrated when Israel passed over Jordan into the Promised Land to receive their inheritance. Notably, Christ repudiated that concept when he told the Jews, "Flesh and blood cannot inherit the kingdom of God." ("That born of the Spirit is Spirit.") As history verifies, Israel's false premise failed to take root and quickly withered. Jerusalem was burned with fire, and the events that swiftly followed proved decisively that an earthy salvation was not an option. Mankind's condition would remain without resolution until the eternal truths imparted to him from on high were seeded into his mind. As the book of Genesis relates, "Now lest the man put forth his hand and eat of the Tree of Life, *the quickening principles that appear in the midst of God's work*, and live forever."

Because the proliferation of temporal darkness within the mind created a communicative veil, symbolized by Moses in the veiling that divided the three chambers within the Lord's tabernacle, it would be to our advantage to closely examine the depths to which this phenomenon extends. In reference to this veiling, Paul asked, "Do you not know that you are the tabernacle of God and that the Spirit of God, *the light of Life*, dwells in you?"

Since it was given to man to inherit all things, the conflict that accompanied the intrusion of darkness into Creation's light surfaced within the psyche. In keeping with that anomaly, the first man, Adam, assumed the role of portraying temporal darkness; and the second man, Christ, assumed the role of portraying God's true light. We should, however, remember that, in the eyes of God, Creation, Christ and man were inseparable. Though outwardly characterized as separate entities, each mirrored the inherent principles that characterized the Creator's person.

Typically, this conflicting anomaly is demonstrated when day and night impose their alternating influences upon the Earth. Beginning with sunset, *the Son's descent,* the darkness of night, *the darkness of temporal thought* conceals what the light of day, *the Son's arrival,* would reveal; and beginning with sunrise, the light of day, *the Son's arrival,* reveals what the darkness of night, *the darkness of temporal thought,* has concealed. Alternately, the one imposes its way upon the other. The inverse dispositions of darkness and light likewise appear in man's religious practices. Because the houses of Judeo-Christian worship place their trust in abstract concepts of heaven for deliverance, their doctrines remain under a veil of darkness. Nevertheless, when that veil is removed, the darkness within their doctrines gives way to the light that resides beyond the veil. ("He has made his light to shine out of darkness.") Since mankind inherently participates in this phenomenon, it is given to all mankind to once experience darkness, but with the Son's arrival they judge in Spirit and in truth. ("When it shall turn to the Lord, the veil shall be taken away.")

Because darkness is void of visible manifestation and signifies the unknown, it mirrors God's condition upon emerging from the dark abyss; and because Christ and man were assigned the role of reconciling the light and darkness within the Creator's work, we should not be surprised to find the principles revealing those two conditions reappearing in Scripture's Word. Since God's Word is the foundation on which Hebrew and Christian theology is built, we see those same conflicting forces resurfacing within their respective houses of worship. Knowing that a veil of darkness has descended upon the entire world, it would be naive to believe that church doctrine could somehow have escaped its effect. The countless divisions that pervade humanity's theological beliefs validate that conclusion. Our purpose here is neither to accuse nor to excuse, but to understand our true relationship to the Creator. Therefore, we should be aware of the dark parallelism that exists between man and his choice of worship, for the dark faces of his secular beliefs are extensions of his own character.

In that regard, Scripture uses dark similes to demonstrate the intrusion of this phenomenon. For instance, God instructed Moses, "Build a tabernacle in the wilderness for me, *a house that replicates the principle of light shining in darkness,* that I may dwell in the midst of the people." With the completion of that pseudo-spiritual edifice, *which the laborers overlaid with skins,* this symbolic house of the Lord journeyed with the people in the wilderness for forty years. During that sojourn all who came out of Egypt perished, with the exception of these three men: Moses, Joshua and Caleb. However, their children lived on to enter the land that was promised to Abraham and his seed. Not unlike those who journeyed in the wilderness with that first tabernacle, few to this day are aware that this painful desert journey remains with us. Our generations also worship the God and the Christ that resides in outer tabernacles, failing to recognize that what they worship is the light of Life that resides within their own midst.

Until we are individually prepared to exit our inherent darkness, we are not ready to welcome the true light that God has imparted to every man, woman and child that comes into the world. The dark side of mankind's religious practices must end. All must be reconciled to God's true light! Jesus spoke of the division that existed between God's revelatory work and the practices of the Hebrew priesthood when he told his disciples, "He that eats bread with me, *the Word's linear reading,* has lifted up his heel against me, *the Word's parallel reading."* Forewarning those who propagate division and false doctrine he said, "A house divided against itself cannot stand." Further reflecting the conflict that existed between himself and mankind's houses of worship, he declared, "Tear down this house that your fathers have built and in three days, *in Spirit and in truth,* I will raise it up!"

As we continue exploring the myriad relationships wherein God has made darkness witness to his light, keep in mind that darkness and light are inherent to all of God's labors. In keeping with that relationship, the psalmist asked:

"Lord, where shall I go to hide from your Spirit? How shall I flee from your presence? If I ascend into heaven, you are there; and if I make my bed in hell, you are there. If I say, Surely the darkness shall cover me, even the light of night shines about me. Indeed, the darkness hides not from you; but it shines as the day. The darkness and the light are both alike before you."

One of the wonders of Scripture is its ability to present God's truth in a multidimensional manner. In that respect, Joseph's life characterizes the various forms of Judeo-Christian worship that continue to this day. Consider the following:

As a Christ type, Joseph received a coat of many colors, *a covering of many colorful truths,* from Jacob, his father. His brethren, influenced by darkness, were jealous and grew very angry. In the heat of their anger, they sold Joseph to traders who carried him away into Egypt's dark land. There, Joseph became a servant in bondage to darkness, *Christ in bondage.*

In time, he was elevated to keeper of the storehouses of Egypt, *keeper of the bread of Life within the dark land.* In performing that role, he laid in the harvest from the years of *Spiritual* plenty to provide for the years of *pseudo-spiritual* famine that God had foretold would befall the dark land.

When the seven years of *pseudo-spiritual* famine arrived as predicted, his brethren came to him for food; which Joseph freely provided. After recognizing that the brother they had sold into bondage was now providing for their needs, the sons of Jacob repented for their ignoble behavior. Joseph then forgave and consoled them, saying, "If you had not sold me into bondage, *valued me for an external reward,* I could not have provided you with bread, *the bread of Life,* for your time of famine."

When Jacob saw God's Way in Joseph, he blessed him saying, "Joseph, *as a simile of Christ in man,* is a fruitful bough whose branches, *whose truths,* reach out to a well, *the well of Life.* His enemies, *man's misconceptions,* have sorely grieved him and shot at him; but his branch abode in strength and his hands were upheld by the Almighty. From henceforth, the shepherd, *the Christ who nourishes his flock,* is the foundation stone, *the Way, the Truth, and the Life,* of Israel."

Just as God's dual nature is characterized in his revelatory work, so the dual nature of Christ and man is characterized in their revelatory work; and because Scripture is an extension of this all-inclusive revelation, that same duality reappears in Judeo-Christian religious practices. The presence of those two witnesses is demonstrated in the following presentations:

Samson, *a Christ type,* went down to Timnath to seek a Philistine woman, *the temporal mind,* for his wife. Along the way, a lion, *the face of a lie, the king of beasts,* challenged him; and he slew it by the Spirit of the Lord that was in him.

When he again returned to Timnath, to take the woman he desired for his wife, he passed by the dead lion and saw a swarm of bees depositing *pseudo-spiritual* honey within its carcass. He then took the honey from within the lion's carcass and ate of it.

When he arrived at Timnath, he mocked the Philistines, *the mind's darkened state,* by asking them to interpret the riddle he was about to put forth. He then spoke this parallelism: "Out of the eater, *the mind's pseudo-spiritual misconceptions,* came forth meat, and out of the strong came forth sweetness." But they could not Spiritually interpret the truth that was hidden in the riddle that was put forth.

Later, in Samson's absence, the Philistines gave Samson's wife, *the pseudo-spiritual mind to which Samson had committed himself,* to one of their own *temporal* kind; and he was very displeased.

Samson therefore captured three hundred foxes, symbolically expressing the mind's three states of reality, and tied firebrands, Spiritual truths, between their two tails. He then turned the foxes loose amongst the fields of the Philistines that awaited harvest. The harvest, of the people in darkness, was thus destroyed and Samson was avenged.

The mind's religious practices are further repudiated when Christ makes his triumphal entry into Jerusalem at the time of Jewish Passover. That assertion reads as follows:

Jesus said to his disciples, "Go into the village that is over against you. There you will find an Ass tied, and a Colt with her. Loose the two and bring them to me. If any man questions your actions you shall say, The Lord has need of them."

This was done that the words of the prophet might be fulfilled, saying, "Behold, your king, *Christ,* comes to you, *to your pseudo-spiritual houses of worship,* meek and sitting upon an Ass, *the Hebrew interpretation of God's pseudo-spiritual Word;*

and upon a Colt, *the Christian interpretation of God's pseudo-spiritual Word, the foal of an Ass."*

We should understand that God's work in its entirety is comprised of symbolic comparisons, and we should not be offended by those comparisons. It is true that God has concluded all things in darkness that he might bring all things into his light. All the law and the prophets embraced and spoke of the darkness that preceded the passage of God's Word into light. The following selections from Scripture are typical:

- "I have come as a light into the world, that you should not abide in darkness."
- "I the Lord have called you, *the Son of man,* in righteousness and I will hold your hand. You shall open the eyes that were blind, and bring those who sit in darkness out from the prison house."
- "As the winter snow and the summer rain come down to water the earth and causes it to bud, that it may give seed to him that sows and bread to him that harvests, so shall the Word that goes forth to reveal my Spirit. It shall not return to me void; but he shall prosper in the work wherein I have sent him."

The symbolism disclosing Christ's presence in the midst of man's prevailing darkness is perhaps one of the most subtle and intriguing of the many parables set forth by Jesus. That parallelism translates as follows:

"When the Son of man comes in his Father's glory, bringing all the holy angels, *all the truths of God,* with him, he shall sit upon the throne of his glory.

All nations, *all that is true or false within the thoughts of men,* shall be gathered before him; and he shall separate them one from another; as a shepherd divides his sheep from the goats. And the sheep, *the true,* shall stand at his right hand and the goats, *the false,* on the left.

And he shall say to those on his right hand, Come, those who are blessed by my Father, inherit the kingdom prepared for you from the foundation of the world.

For, I was hungry, and you gave me meat. *You nourished the soul's true light.* I was thirsty, and you gave me to drink. *You gave water from the well of Life to the soul's true light.* I was a stranger, and you took me in. *You provided a haven within yourself for the soul's true light.*

I was naked and you clothed me. *You clothed the soul's true light with Spiritual attire.* I was sick and you visited me. *You gave solace and reassurance to the soul's true light.* I was in prison and you came to me. *You sought release for the soul's true light.*

Then shall the righteous ask him, When did we do all these things with you? And the Son of man shall reply, Inasmuch that you have done it unto one of the least of these my brethren, *one of the least of these who seek Spiritual truth,* you did it unto me."

In viewing the soul's true light as Christ's brethren, an additional aspect of man's character comes to light. Having previously shown that the inherent truths within God's work are equal to the angels of heaven, if we accept Christ's parallelism that "the children of the resurrection are equal to the angels of heaven," we must then conclude that the mind of Christ is equal to the angels, or the truths, of heaven. That is, the sum of God's angels within the mind comprises the body of Christ. Therefore, those who attain "the mind of Christ" become "equal to the angels of heaven." Scripture supports this interpretation by way of an antithesis, when the apostle relates, "The angels, *the pseudo-spiritual principles of men,* that kept not their first estate, *their true heritage in God,* but left their habitations, has he reserved in darkness unto the judgment of that great day, w*hen the mind is led into all truth.*"

Because the Father of lights has patterned all things after his own image and likeness, his myriad faces appear throughout the Universe. Joyfully, Christ and man have inherited the same. Therefore, he that has seen the true light within his own face has seen the true light within Christ's face; and he that has seen the true light within Christ's face has seen the true light within the principles that reveal God's face. As the Book of Revelation relates, "They shall see his face and his name, *his knowledge,* shall be written in their foreheads." Therein, the everlasting glory that shines within all that God has made is unveiled.

5

Resurrection

"We who knew not the truth, but resided in darkness, has he quickened together to sit in heavenly places with Christ Jesus."

ROMANS 6:5

When Jesus came teaching his message of salvation to the Jews, he knew their redemption hinged upon "the resurrection of the body," upon translating the Word's pseudo-spiritual truth from external darkness into internal light. He therefore taught, "He that saves his life, *he that clings to his temporal interpretations of life,* shall lose it, *shall lose its Spiritual truth;* but he that loses his life for my sake, *for the sake of the true light which is his eternal heritage,* shall save it unto life eternal." However, to the Jews of that era, resurrection of the body implied resurrection of their physical form from the grave. Having misconstrued Christ's message, the Jewish clergy promptly rejected his teachings, even though they were Spiritually rooted in the law and the prophets. ("If you had believed Moses and the prophets you would have known me, for they spoke of me.") Unlike their predecessors, today's Christians believe in the resurrection of the body — life after death — but as the offspring of Judaism, they too fail to understand what the word "resurrection" Spiritually implies. They therefore err in teaching that salvation precedes resurrection. They contend that salvation is immediately available but associate Christ's resurrection with life beyond the grave. They fail to understand that man is without salvation until after his pseudo-spiritual mind is raised from its dead misconceptions. By externalizing Christ's message, the concept of an internal resurrection is again lost and Christ's promises to all nations are made of non-effect. ("You make the Word of God of non-effect by your tradition.")

Having failed to understand that knowing God through Christ fulfills the body's Spiritual resurrection, *the resurrection of God's living Word,* both Judaism and Christianity have placed life eternal beyond man's grasp. ("I am the resurrection and the Life. He that comes to me, *to my eternal truth,* though he were dead, *through pseudo-spiritual error,* yet shall he live.") We must cease from circumventing God's revelatory instruction and replacing its truth with the misguided beliefs to which mankind has fallen prey. The time for understanding that life and death are in the world as living states of reality is long overdue. Two thousand years ago, Jesus told his disciples, "You shall not have gone through the cities of Judea before the Son of man has come in his Father's kingdom." His assurance of the kingdom's immanent arrival correlates with his earlier disclosure, "My Father's kingdom, *the kingdom of God,* is within you. My Father's Spirit, *the kingdom of heaven,* is among you." Thus, when the Son of man comes in his Father's kingdom, he reappears in man as an extension of his Father's Spirit. Unable to accept the immediate availability of this all-inclusive unity, both Jew and Christian continue to look for signs of the Messiah's promised return, *Christ's second coming,* but no sign is given. Mirroring the words of the false prophet Baal, they would behold him, but not now. They would see him, but not nigh. As Paul relates, "They could not enter in because of unbelief."

The mystery so long associated with resurrection is quickly resolved once the soul's passage from the death of pseudo-spiritual belief to the Life of Spiritual understanding is accomplished.

By Spiritual definition, "resurrection" is the eliminating of mankind's dead misconceptions; the quickening of a body of thought that was previously void of knowing God's eternal truth. ("I am the resurrection and the Life. He that comes to me, though he were dead, yet shall he live.")

Since the Bible views temporal darkness as death, and because the mind's first two states of reality are afflicted by temporal darkness, man's first two levels of comprehension are viewed as states of living death. Deliverance from this living death constitutes the mind's first and second resurrections. Jesus spoke of obtaining resurrection through the Spiritual light that was in him when he told the Jews, "I have come as a light into the world that you should not abide in darkness." Identifying himself with the empowering principles of resurrection, he declared, "I have power to lay down my life and I have power to take it up again." In like manner, mankind has the power to lay down his life of pseudo-spiritual error and to raise it up again in Spirit and in truth.

The certainty that man's passage from temporal darkness into Spiritual light constitutes resurrection is set forth when Christ correlates, "As the Father, *through his signs and wonders,* raises up the dead and quickens them, so has he given to the Son, *through his signs and wonders,* to quicken whom he will." Fulfilling resurrection through the conversion of similes is also applicable to the advent of primordial Creation. For when the dark void is equated to death and the emerging light is equated to Life, it translates, "As the Father gave Life to what was void in the abyss, so has he given to the Son to give Life to what was void in man." ("I do only those things I see with the Father.") Since all is initially conceived in a voidal state, all must be passed from death unto Life.

Because the psyche's temporal and pseudo-spiritual realities are rooted in outer darkness, *judgment by appearance,* their promised redemption is obviously dependent upon achieving a new and higher form of comprehension. ("A better resurrection.") Christ referred to this higher calling when he explained, "No man has ascended into heaven except he that came down from heaven, even the Son of man which is in heaven." That is, "No man has entered into the Spirit of God except he that is born of the Spirit of God, even the Son of man who is in the Spirit of God." Notice that he did not say everyone who prayed, "Lord! Lord!" would ascend into heaven. As he told the Jews, "Your fathers did eat manna, *temporal knowledge,* in the desert and they are dead, *their generations remain in darkness to this day.* I am that manna, *that Spiritual knowledge,* which comes down from heaven, *comes down from the Father of lights,* that a man may eat of and not die, *may eat of and not remain in darkness.*" In the same context he told his disciples, "You must eat my flesh and drink my blood, *you must share in my body of Spiritual knowledge,* or you have no Life in you."

Paul recognized the importance of the mind's unity with Christ's Spiritual knowledge when he wrote, "Let this mind, *this knowledge,* be in you that was also in Christ Jesus." And again when he counseled, "Be transformed by the renewing of your mind, *by renewing your understanding of The Eternal.*" In light of the profile imparted to man when God said, "Let us make man in our image and after our likeness," Paul recognized that the time had come for man to personalize the heritage that God had given him, to experience the Ultimate Reality of sharing Christ's eternal light, *the Son of man's "second resurrection."*

Since all that the law and the prophets had witnessed referred to Christ, man would need to transpose the Word's instructional signs and wonders and reconcile their Spiritual content to himself, *rather than perceiving those analogies as historical or moral directives,* before he would achieve resurrection. Only then would his glorification in the body of Christ be realized and his entry into the kingdom of heaven be fulfilled. ("I am the true vine, *the true light,* you are the branches. Abide in me for the branch cannot bear fruit except it abide in the vine, *except it abide in the true light.")*

The mind's ability to raise the dead, *to interpret and give Life to the Word's latent similes,* is inherent and is demonstrated in the following example:

If we were handed a message that read, "The door is open!" the words would remain lifeless until they were transposed and quickened within the mind. The message would then come to life and the knowledge it conveyed would become part of our reality.

The same is true of Scripture's two readings. Each reading must be transposed and quickened by the mind before it achieves reality. How that reading is interpreted will depend upon the individual's level of perception.

With the quickening of the Word's second reading, *the conversion of its message through paralleling,* the veil present at the first reading, *the Word's linear or traditional reading,* is removed, and the psyche is passed from its previous state of pseudo-spiritual death into God's promised light of Life.

It is important to understand in making this transition that God's Word is dimensional and progressive. Therefore, the mind's ability to change its perception proceeds incrementally and can be Spiritually enlightened only to the degree that the reader is prepared to accept. ("What you bind in earth shall be bound in heaven, and what you release in earth shall be released in heaven.") Thus, like most tasks, mankind's Spiritual renewal becomes a work in progress.

In concert with this passover of cognizance, Paul correctly emphasized that man's mortal faith had its limitations, that "faith without works is dead." Jesus acknowledged the same when he instructed his disciples, "Labor not for the meat that perishes but for the meat that endures unto life eternal." Many have faith in God and believe in Christ but are totally unaware that faith and belief belong to the realm of those who have yet to receive the promise of life eternal. As John's Gospel relates, "To as many as *Spiritually* believed on him, to them gave he the *quickening* power to become the Sons of God." Chiding the Jews for their unbelief, Christ criticized their loyalty to traditional will-worship, saying, "Search the Scriptures, for in them you think you have life; and they are they that testify of me. But you will not come to me, *you will not come to the light of my knowledge,* that you might have life." No man can know God by making faith or belief an end in itself. Until we give ourselves to understanding Spiritual truth, our faith remains dead. As the apostle emphasized, "Show me your works and I will know your faith by your works." ("By their fruits you shall know them.")

Having recognized that our reality is directly related to our knowledge, and that the mind is characterized by how it interprets that knowledge, we can readily see how Spiritual perception is critical to accomplishing resurrection. The importance of understanding Spiritual conversion is clearly demonstrated at Golgotha when the thief on the cross, *a simile of the pseudo-spiritual mind,* pleads, "Lord, remember me, *Spiritually renew my members,* when you come in your kingdom." And Christ replies,

"This day you shall be with me in Paradise." By using that climactic event to reveal the immediacy of the second resurrection of God's Word, Christ again corroborates the promised translation of the pseudo-spiritual mind into God's Paradise kingdom. He implies the same when he counsels his disciples, "A little while and the world shall see me, *externally,* no more. But you shall see me, *internally,* and because I live, *in Spirit and in truth,* you shall live also." To erase any confusion over Scripture's view of man's "two deaths," "two resurrections," and "two judgments," you will find the following explanation enlightening.

The first death is expressed as the mind's temporal, or pseudo-spiritual, darkness. That death is initially identified when the apostle writes, "Death reigned from Adam until Moses." Regarding the apostle's timing, the following factors should be taken into account:

While Moses is credited with writing the first five books of the Bible, the similes recorded on those pages had yet to be interpreted and understood. It was not until the Creator's Word was conveyed to Israel on two tablets of stone at Sinai that knowledge directly relating mankind to God's Spirit was received. This transferring of power to Abraham's seed signaled the approaching hour of man's "first resurrection."

However, when the children of Israel fashioned the golden calf, they negated "the first resurrection." The first death thus remained in place and was symbolized when Moses broke the first two tablets of instruction received on the mount. Thereafter, the pseudo-spiritual mind characterized not only the failure of the "first resurrection" but also signaled the continuation of the "first death," *an earthy concept of self-reliance that dated back to Adam and Eve.*

Accordingly, the conflicting forces of darkness that appeared in mankind's temporal and pseudo-spiritual thought were extended to God's Word. What the Creator had intended to reveal of himself at Sinai was made of non-effect. God's initial effort to make his light in mankind to shine out of darkness had failed.

With the mixing of the mind's first two levels of consciousness, the need for a "first resurrection" dramatically increased. Nonetheless, that Spiritual quickening would be held in abeyance until the prophet Elijah had Spiritually transposed the pseudo-spiritual aspect of the law received at Sinai and was taken up into heaven. Concurring with that event, Elijah would reappear within the prophets as the Son of man, and thereafter all the prophets would witness to his eternal presence. Through Elijah's ability to translate and personify God's Word within the human frame, the first death was thus overcome and a "first resurrection" was attained. As Paul relates, "Through death, *through eliminating the temporal elements that intruded into the pseudo-spiritual mind,* he overcame him who had the power of death." This event is further demonstrated when God nullifies his first covenant and replaces it with a second covenant. The same is witnessed when the Word's first reading is replaced by a second reading. Accordingly, he that has the glorified body of Elijah, *the Son of man,* within himself has experienced the "first resurrection." By raising the mind's pseudo-spiritual level of comprehension to a Spiritual level, the first death was thus overcome and had no further effect upon the Spiritually changed psyche.

Paul introduces us to the era of Christ's death, *the death of God's Word through further misinterpretation,* and forthcoming "second resurrection" when he writes:

"If we are buried in the likeness of Christ's death, *if we recognize our death in the Word's first reading,* we shall appear with him in the likeness of his resurrection, *when mind and body are Spiritually transposed and reappear with him in the Word's second reading."* Therein, all is Spiritually raised and passed from death unto Life.

We thus see a "first resurrection" accomplished through the transposing of the law of Moses into the Word-body of the Son of man and a "second resurrection" accomplished through the transposing of prophesy into the Word-body of Jesus Christ. ("I have glorified you and I will glorify you again.") Through these two resurrections, mind and body Spiritually ascend to the Father, and in that ascent, the Christ in man sits with God in heavenly places. ("I will receive you unto myself.")

When Jesus spoke of the resurrection of the dead, he said that nothing would be lost but the son of perdition, the temporal error that, when removed from God's work, transposes pseudo-spiritual knowledge into Spiritual understanding. For sure, you cannot save a lie or an illusion, something that is not and yet is. As for the psyche's three levels of reality, in the resurrection what is temporal remains temporal, what is pseudo-spiritual remains pseudo-spiritual, and what is Spiritual remains Spiritual. As promised, man inherits all things, and therein all things are judged. ("He that overcomes shall inherit all things.")

In regard to the "second death," those who have refused the Spiritual counsel that pervades the Word-body of the Son of man, or those who have refused the Spiritual counsel that pervades the Word-body of Christ, the same remain in the "second death." They have refused all knowledge relating to the Spirit of the living God. As Paul relates, "They are without hope, *by choice, twice dead.*"

This brings us to Scripture's disclosure of a first and last judgment. The apostle refers to these two forms of judgment when he writes, "As in the first man, Adam, all men die, so in Christ all are made alive." In concert with the foregoing summaries, the temporal and pseudo-spiritual minds are limited to making "reasonable judgments." These first two levels of comprehension comprise the "first judgment." In contrast, the Spiritual mind judges in Spirit and in truth and is ordered by the Creator's inherent principles. The myriad truths that witness to man in this enlightened state of comprehension comprise the "last judgment."

Many of those who ascribe to knowledge relating to the first judgment live in fear of an afterlife that threatens hell fire and damnation. They fail to understand that fire is a symbol employed by Scripture to describe the purging of temporal error from the pseudo-spiritual mind. ("Fire came down from God out of heaven and destroyed them all.") Not to be feared, this purging of errors is accompanied by fiery truths that define the resurrection experience. ("When the Father's truth within Christ had purged our errors, he sat down at the right hand of the majesty on high.") Referring to this purging of misconceptions by fire, the Book of Revelation relates, "No unclean thing shall enter in, neither that which works abomination or makes a lie; but those whose names are written in heaven's Book of Life, *those whose knowledge lives in Spirit and in truth.*"

From these disclosures, we should now understand that the resurrection of the body refers to the resurrection of Christ's body, the resurrection of that body of knowledge that conveys the Spiritual principles of God to man. When we Spiritually unite with that body of eternal truth, we become one with the Christ who was dead, *whose knowledge was dead through mankind's misconceptions,* and is alive forevermore. Having received the power to become Sons of God, *and Co-Creators with God,* we pass over that threshold wherein all things become new, and therein we find Christ's promised power and glory inwardly fulfilled. ("All power is given to me in heaven and earth.")

6

The Name of the Lord

"I tell you now: You shall not see me again, until you shall say, Blessed is he that comes in the name of the Lord."

MATTHEW 23:39

One of the most perplexing subjects I encountered when I first began to seriously study Scripture was what Jesus meant when he said, "Whatever you ask of the Father in my name he will give you." What further confused me was the fact that people in all walks of life were praying to God and asking to have their prayers answered "in Jesus name" but comparatively few ever received a positive response. The explanation offered by the clergy for this void in communication was that God had their best interest at heart and that God's reply was, "No." As it turned out, that viewpoint was only partially correct. Since Christ always presented the Father in a positive light, the torrent of "No" replies and the scarcity of "Yes" replies disturbed me. Within my heart, I knew something was wrong. There had to be another explanation.

The disciple James was likewise troubled over God's lack of response and explained to his followers, "You ask and receive not because you ask amiss: you ask for things to satisfy your personal lusts and desires." Then, as now, people were only concerned with fulfilling their immediate earthly needs. They took no thought for what God desired for them. Jesus warned of this self-serving attitude, when he said, "As it was in the days of Noah, so shall it be in the days of the Son of man. They were eating and drinking, marrying and giving in marriage, until the flood came and took them all away." We do not need to look far to see that riotous living is still mankind's major pastime.

It is amazing how some things never change. When we read that Christ told his followers, "The things that I do you shall do also," his miracles immediately come to mind. Everyone wants to perform miracles, but not on themselves. They envision the adulation that comes with the gift of healing, but few are prepared to first heal their own imperfections. In short, they are unwilling to follow Christ's lead. ("I have come not to do my own will but the will of him that sent me.") The psalmist understood this Spiritual prerequisite when he wrote, "In the volume of the book it is written of me, I come O Lord to do your will." When I considered this conflict of interest, it became painfully clear that while people expected to receive gifts in Christ's name, paying the price for what was his was far removed from their minds. As the prophet expressed it, "This people draws near to me with their mouth and confesses me with their lips, but their heart is far from me."

Perhaps the greatest difficulty encountered in asking for gifts in Christ's name is that the petitioner fails to understand what their request entails. When we ask to receive something in Christ's name, we are actually requesting a change of personal identity, we are asking to become one with God, even as Christ is one with God. ("The Father and I are one.") This involves a relinquishing of the temporal self, a prerequisite annunciated when Jesus said, "He that seeks his life must lose it." If the treasures of

God are embodied in Christ, and if those treasures are to be man's eternal heritage, then to receive their reward we must unite with the mind of Christ. We cannot serve two masters. ("Where your treasure is, there will your heart be also.") Not having the faintest idea of what asking for gifts in Christ's name involved, it is no wonder that mankind continues to ask amiss.

One of the most disturbing aspects of humanity is that everyone wants to be successful on their own terms. Obviously, that is impossible. No man ever became Spiritually adept on his own. As Jesus said, "It is the Father within me that does the work." Sooner or later, we must all learn that no matter how hard we try, we cannot fill life's glass without the aid of God. Many have tried, unsuccessfully, to accomplish that task. As an alternative to failure, they have tried filling the glass half-full, *as in the half-filled glass of the pseudo-spiritual mind.* But that too was unsuccessful, for the emptiness in the glass reflects their personal insufficiency, and they ponder the loss of what might have been.

An example of mankind being satisfied with a half-filled glass is typically demonstrated at Hebrew and Christian weddings. In those symbolic ceremonies, the uniting of the bride and groom signifies the uniting of the Word's two aspects, the pseudo-spiritual representing the bride and the Spiritual representing the groom. ("His bride has made herself ready.") Mirroring Scripture's pattern, after the two principals have vowed to give themselves to each other, the bride's pseudo-spiritual veil is removed. With the veil taken away, the two come face to face with each other's true features, and they embrace. As one, they are then Spiritually united. ("What God has joined together, let no man put asunder.") Since those in attendance are witnesses to their union, all go forth into the wedding feast "in the name of the Lord." But, regrettably, at most traditional weddings, neither the bride nor the groom, nor those in attendance, have the slightest inkling of the Spiritual truths witnessed at the wedding ceremony. Their glass therefore remains only half full.

In a comparable scenario, once those in attendance are assembled at the wedding feast, the best man, *he that witnesses to the Son of man,* honors the bride and groom with a toast pledging their future happiness. Symbolically, he drinks the wine and breaks the glass. Again, this custom mirrors Scripture's pattern. The wine of Life represents God's truth. The glass symbolizes the Spiritual Word, *the transparent vessel,* which holds the wine. Once the wine, *God's truth,* is ingested, the vessel, *the Word's transparency,* is broken and all attending the wedding feast glory at the uniting of the bride and groom. However, on a temporal level, those present at the wedding feast are caught up in the revelry of the moment. In seeing they see not, and in hearing they hear not. Their Spiritual reward in Christ's name is therefore lost.

One of the psyche's most phenomenal attributes is its ability to accomplish reformation through knowledge. That process begins at birth. At that time, the parents provide their child with a "given name." That given name, however, is not the child's true identity. That identity will be formed by the knowledge gathered as the child grows. Since all children interpret life through their senses, all come in their own name, in their own interpretation of the knowledge they have gathered. Notwithstanding, knowledge and its accompanying reality are transitional. Therefore, as the mind exercises its transitory powers, the knowledge it has gathered passes from one level of understanding to another. ("When I was a child I thought as a child but when I became a man I put away childish things.")

As the psyche evolves, it ultimately discovers the path leading to Spiritual rebirth. If it continues to go forward, it will become a New Creation and be provided with "a new name." ("Upon him that overcomes I will write my new name, *my new knowledge.*") And in that new knowledge the psyche comes in the name of the Lord. ("Blessed is he that comes in the name of the Lord.")

All of Scripture's prophets walked this path and came to Israel in the name of the Lord. ("Thus says the Lord.") They identified their new Spiritual knowledge as God's true light and said of that light, "His name shall be called Immanuel;" God with us. *He shall be with us as God's embodied knowledge.* As the Book of Revelation recounts, "Behold, the Tabernacle of God is with men." Later, when the Son of man told his disciples, "I am the Truth, the Way and the Life. No man comes to the Father except by me," he said in effect, "My knowledge discloses the Father's Truth, my knowledge discloses the Father's Way, and my knowledge discloses the Father's Life. No man comes to the Father except by my knowledge." Thus, to enter into the name of the Lord, the psyche must acquire Christ's knowledge. And those who acquire that knowledge come "in the name of the Lord." They have attained unity with God.

Once we understand that the name of the Lord refers to God's knowledge of himself embodied in Christ, what we ask "in Jesus' Name" takes on a completely new meaning. From the very beginning, all Creation became an outpicturing of God's knowledge of himself. All that appeared came in the name of the Lord. This was the Creator's true light, the same true light that lights every man coming into the world. The same true light that awaits resurrection from the dark recesses of the mind and body. Paul referred to the everlasting presence of this inherent light when he exhorted his companion, Timothy, "Stir up the gift that is in you." Indeed, this was the gift imparted to man in the beginning, when God said, "Let us make man in our image and after our likeness." And this was the gift that Adam and Eve forfeited in Eden.

The difference between the man that comes in his own name, *in his own knowledge,* and he that comes in the name of the Lord, *in the knowledge of the Lord,* appears in the following:

- ■ "If the heart of any man or woman shall turn away from the Lord, he shall blot their name, *their knowledge,* out of heaven."
- ■ "If you had followed my counsel and listened to my instruction I would have extended peace like a river to you; and your name, *your knowledge,* would not have been cut off and destroyed before me."
- ■ "The light of the wicked shall be put out. His remembrance shall perish from the earth. His name, *his knowledge,* shall no more be found in the street."
- ■ "You have rebuked the heathen and destroyed the wicked. You have put out their name, *their knowledge,* forever."
- ■ "He shall not be held guiltless that takes the name of the Lord, *the knowledge of the Lord,* in vain."

Compare the above with the following quotations, which indicate the mind's Spiritual entry into the name of the Lord.

- ■ "His name, *his knowledge,* shall endure forever; it shall outshine the sun. Let the whole earth be filled with his glory."
- ■ "The government shall be upon his shoulder; and his name, *his knowledge,* shall be called Wonderful, Counselor, The Mighty God, the Everlasting Father, the Prince of Peace."
- ■ "In that day there shall be one Lord; and those who enter into his name, *who enter into his knowledge,* shall be one."
- ■ "The hand of the Lord is upon the Son of man, whom he has made for himself. Quicken us, O Lord, and we will call upon your name, *we will walk in the light of your knowledge.*"
- ■ "He was clothed in a vesture dipped in blood, *dipped in truth,* and his name, *his knowledge,* is called the Word of God."

Having considered these examples, it should be clear to all that two distinct forms of knowledge exist. Too, we should understand that entry into this higher knowledge can only be achieved through unity with God's Spirit.

Perhaps the next time we pray the Father in Jesus' name, we will be better prepared to receive his answer, to receive the gift he so willingly gives; namely, himself! ("It is my Father's good pleasure to give you his kingdom.")

7

Judgment

"I watched until the Ancient of Days was enthroned;
and I saw the likeness of a fiery stream, of Spiritual
truth, issuing before him.

Thousands upon thousands, of similes, ministered
to him and countless numbers stood before him.

The judgment was set and the books were
opened."

DANIEL 7:10

When the Creator formed the visible worlds, he had one purpose in mind. He wanted to establish judgment. ("All the ways of God are judgment.") But he did not foresee the conflict that would accompany his efforts. When Creation's first light appeared, two different types of judgment also appeared. The void had brought forth after its own kind and darkness was infused into God's quickened light. Inadvertently, the Creator had given Life to both primal darkness and primal light. Two distinct types of Creation and two distinct types of knowledge thereafter appeared in all that God made. As two in one body, the darkness witnessed to the void wherein it was formed and the light witnessed to the Life wherein it was quickened. The one was rooted in Creation's ever-changing appearance, the other was rooted in Creation's never-changing Source. Knowing this, Jesus cautioned, "Judge not according to the appearance; but judge right judgment."

Creation thus appeared as a work in conflict, a work divided against itself. Notwithstanding, over countless eons of time, life's myriad manifestations evolved into that unfathomable expanse that comprises the Cosmos. Meanwhile, on earth, a new Age was being born. The primates were progressively acquiring the skills of self-survival and were attaining a semi-intelligent form of comprehension. In time, primordial man emerged, having a higher level of cognizance than anything previously created. And God conceived a way to utilize man's comprehensive ability. Endowing him with the faculty of Reason, he fashioned his body as a vehicle capable of reconciling the darkness and division that encroached upon his work.

To further his vision of providing Creation with a unifying glory, the Creator provided "Adam" with sensory faculties capable of transposing visible Creation into the invisible principles that supported his work. As a microcosm of all things preceding him, man was then assigned the role of God's reconciling vehicle. To advance this endeavor he provided subsequent generations with instructional signs and wonders, similes designed to enhance man's ability to reconcile the darkness that impaired his work. Mirroring the pattern set forth by Moses in the Creation analogy, God set two great lights within his similes to give light upon the earth. The greater light, *his internal light* to rule the day and the lesser light, *his external light,* to rule the night. If all went as planned, when man recognized the true light that appeared within the Creator's work, he would begin reconciling the two great lights to himself. Through that labor, the darkness and division that impaired Creation would be dispelled.

Early man thus obtained discretionary judgment. Through

the inverse flow of cognizance provided by the body's sensory faculties, he was capable of transposing Creation's visible substance, *the Tree of Knowledge of good and evil,* into invisible consciousness. Conversely, he could transpose Creation's invisible substance, *the Tree of Life,* into visible manifestation, a*s seen in Spiritual thought, in comprehensive speech, or more currently, in probing microscopic life forms.* He was thus given the ability to judge the visible and invisible things of heaven and earth. As Christ disclosed, "The Father has committed all judgment to the Son." Accordingly, the light within man's spirit was predestined to know all things, to understand all things and to judge all things. Upon recognizing mankind's reconciling role, the prophet asserted, "He shall raise up the waste places and repair the foundations of old; and he shall be called, the repairer of the breach."

While the mind's capacity to judge is viewed by science as an evolutionary miracle, from a Spiritual viewpoint judgment is considered God's ultimate effort to establish his everlasting glory. When the Creator gave Adam the potential for unlimited judgment, his purpose was twofold. First, he would use man to characterize Creation's darkness. Then, in a progressive manner, he would use signs and wonders to raise man's consciousness to an ultimate level of comprehension. Thereby, the Creator would divide the light from the darkness and overcome the dark misconceptions that intruded into his work. Once the anomaly of darkness was removed, man and the light of Life, which is the Source of all reality, would obtain true judgment. Man, in conjunction with the Christ who resided within his midst, was thus preordained to become God's reconciling instrument. ("Having reconciled all things unto himself, he sat down at the right hand of the majesty on high.")

In exploring the various facets of judgment, we should be eminently aware that the darkness that emerged with Creation's first light would historically be characterized as Christ in bondage. This analogy is expressed by Scripture as "the lamb of God, *the light of Life,* that was slain, *that suffered darkness and death,* from the foundation of the world." Thus, with the forming of Adam as a microcosm of all things preceding him, Christ's inherent dark bondage was imparted to man and all awaited liberation from the intruding darkness that signified God's primordial state. Some four thousand years after Moses had written the Book of Genesis, the apostle would recount, "The whole Creation groans and travails in pain until now, awaiting the glorious manifestation of the Sons of God, *the glorious uniting of God, Christ and Man in one, all-inclusive, Collective Consciousness.*"

Today, with that unifying work completed, the dark judgment that initially afflicted the Word's first reading is removed. To those who sincerely seek God's truth a second reading appears, a reading wherein his true light shines through in all its glory. ("To him that overcomes I will give to eat of the hidden manna.") As evidenced in this change in perception, when the books of the Bible are read as historical or moral timeline accounts, their words fall upon the mind like clouds without water and like seed that is sown in stony places. What Spiritually pertains to the reader is thus lost. Nonetheless, when the timeline is removed from the Word's first reading, all is recognized as residing in the eternal. ("I have come to seek and to save that which was lost.")

In light of these disclosures, it would not be plausible to speak of Christ in bondage without inferring that, in the beginning, God also emerged from the abyss in bondage. ("The Father and I are one.") We therefore find God, and by extension, Creation, being afflicted by darkness before attaining their true light. The concept of darkness preceding light dates back to the Creation analogy provided by Genesis, which reads, "And God divided the light from the darkness; and the evening and the morning were the first day." Accordingly, mankind's first and second levels of judgment begin in darkness, and thereafter emerge from their voidal state into Life's true light. All manifestation is thus recognized as beginning on a temporal level and evolving before attaining Spiritual unity and true judgment.

As the Creator's use of signs and wonders to convey eternal principles progressed, he finally succeeded in separating his true light in Adam from the darkness that intruded into his work. And the eternal glory that God's light revealed was infinitely greater than the dark reality that previously clouded all that he had made. ("The glory of this latter house shall be greater than the former.") In this highly enlightened state, man became "the brightness of the Father's glory and the express image of his person." Indeed, all that the Creator had made witnessed to his all-inclusive unity. ("The morning stars sang together and all the Sons of God shouted for joy.") The labor of achieving true Spiritual judgment had, after countless generations of failure, finally come to fruition. There was none lost but the son of perdition, the anomaly of darkness conceived by the mind while in its temporal and pseudo-spiritual states.

When Genesis relates, "Let us make man in our image and after our likeness," the words "us" and "our" primarily relate to the combined presence of God and Christ within created form. Since man is also embodied in created form, the precedent of darkness that was set before his inception predetermined that his sojourn through life would begin in bondage. However, with the advent of his translation into the "Son of man," that inherent division was overcome. Scripture expresses that Spiritual transition as follows:

■ "The first man, Adam, *Christ in bondage,* was made a living soul. The second man, Adam, *Christ glorified,* was made a quickening Spirit."

- "What is man, *Christ in bondage,* that you are mindful of him, and the Son of man, *Christ glorified,* that you visit him."
- "The first man, *Christ in bondage,* is of the earth, earthy; the second man, *Christ glorified,* is the Lord from heaven."
- "As in Adam, *Christ in bondage,* all men die, so in Christ, *Christ glorified,* all are made alive."
- "You that have been with me in the regeneration, *Christ glorified,* shall sit upon twelve thrones and judge the twelve tribes of Israel, *Christ in bondage.*"

Verifying this pattern, the psalmist writes, "Lord, if I ascend into heaven you are there, *Christ glorified,* and if I make my bed in hell you are there, *Christ in bondage.*" The book of Revelation then adds, "Upon him that overcomes, *Christ in bondage,* I will write my new name, *Christ glorified.*" In this, we further confirm that Christ personified the true light in all that God had made.

Since Life's basic principle prescribes that all things must bring forth after their own kind, it follows that in characterizing Christ as the true light that emerged from the abyss at Creation's inception, we must likewise characterize the darkness that emerged with him at that time. That dark entity is identified throughout Christianity as the Antichrist. The following similes are typical of those used by Scripture to portray the power of the Antichrist to deceive:

- "The Prince of this world comes and he has nothing in me."
- "The Devil was a murderer from the beginning, for there is no truth in him. When he speaks a lie he speaks of his own; for he is a liar and the father of it."
- "The dead bodies of my two witnesses shall lie in the streets of that great city which is called Sodom and Egypt; where also where our Lord was crucified — Golgotha — by *interpretation, 'the place of the skull.'*"

- "And upon her forehead was a name written, Mystery, Babylon the Great. The Mother of Harlots and Abominations of the Earth."
- "Many false prophets shall arise and deceive many, and because inequity shall abound the loves of many shall wax cold."
- "And that Old Serpent, called The Devil and Satan, was cast out of heaven; and his angels were cast out with him."

Rebuking the pseudo-spiritual mind for participating in deceptive religious practices, Christ scolded the Jews, "If the light in you, *the signs and wonders of God that are witnessed in you*, creates only darkness, then your darkness is great."

While our attention is focused on the anomaly of Antichrist, the role of this illusory power to distort eternal truth should be emphasized. Since all communication is based upon symbolism, Scripture employs diverse types of imagery to characterize the deceptive nature of this entity. Setting those characterizations within a time frame, John's Revelation refers to the illusory Antichrist as something that was, is not, and yet is. Its ability to deceive is typically demonstrated when Moses ascends the mount to receive the Commandments of God. While Moses is on the mount, the children of Israel err in judgment and fashion the Golden Calf, a symbol of pagan worship. By assigning power to this abstraction, the sons of Jacob, without forethought, disgrace themselves before God.

There is no question that mankind today unknowingly bows to figments of his imagination, to deceptive thoughts equal to those of previous generations. Although the faces of will-worship change with time, the affect upon humanity's judgment remains the same. Indeed, it is said that the world is never so divided as when people enter their houses of worship on the Sabbath day. This divisiveness accomplishes nothing. What is false cannot alter what is eternally true. As Christ explained, "The prince of this world comes and he has nothing in me."

Nonetheless, rampant deception afflicts mankind to this day. Referring to the gross darkness that continually impedes the psyche, John writes, "He, *the light of Life,* was in the world, and the world was made by him, and the world knew him not. He came unto his own, *clothed in instructional signs and wonders,* and his own received him not." Jesus likewise warned of present and future deception saying, "Watch! For you know not at what hour the Son of man shall come. If the good man of the house had known at what hour the thief would come, he would not have allowed him to break in and spoil his goods."

On a more positive note, since the signs and wonders that comprise God's Word were imparted to mankind for judgmental purposes, namely, the perfecting of the Father's eternal glory, we find expressions of their importance appearing throughout the Bible. The following are examples:

- "Lord, who besides you has the Word of Life?" *Words of true judgment.*
- "The words that I speak are Spirit, and they are Life." *Words of true judgment.*
- "The word, *the judgment,* which you hear is not mine, but the Father's which sent me."
- "Now you are clean through the word, *the judgment,* which I have spoken to you. Abide in me, for the branch cannot bear fruit except it abide in the vine."
- "By your words, *in true judgment,* you shall be justified or by your words, *in false judgment,* you shall be condemned."
- You shall give account for every word, *every judgment,* that proceeds out of your mouth."
- "Your Word, *your judgment,* O Lord, is a light unto my path, a lamp unto my feet."

Clearly, the Bible's message in its entirety centers on two forms of judgment, each interpretive level relating to the two aspects of God's Person. Not unlike the bush that burned at Sinai and was not consumed, God's greater and lesser lights burn brightly in man today, but we must turn aside from humanity's timeworn path of abstract will-worship if we are to find the eternal truths that God has conveyed to us.

Conclusively, there is a first and last judgment. There is a temporal judgment that is external and there is a Spiritual judgment that is internal. There is a judgment that witnesses to darkness and a judgment that witnesses to light. ("I am the first and the last, said the Lord.") When Jesus said, "For judgment I am come; that those who see not might see," he inferred that man could only know God by committing his thoughts to the true light that was in him. To inherit this higher calling, however, man would need to embrace what former generations had refused to consider; namely, to adopt the spirit of reconciliation and thereby reconcile eternal truth unto himself. ("He has given to us the Spirit of reconciliation; whereby we cry, My Father! My God!") Only then would his estrangement from all things eternal come to an end.

A wise man once wrote, "Ignorance shall continue until it wearies of itself." It is a sad, but true, commentary. One that all of humanity should take to heart.

8

Glory

"Father, I have given them the words that you gave to me; and they have received them.

And the glory that you gave to me I have given to them, that they may be one, even as we are one."

JOHN 17:8,22

Exactly why people think of God's glory as otherworldly is a mystery to me. Jesus neither thought, nor taught, any such thing. Contrarily, he openly demonstrated the knowledge and glory of God that was in him and prayed that those who believed on him receive the same. ("Father, I would that those you have given me be with me where I am; that they may behold the glory you have given me.") The only plausible explanation for man's assumption that God's glory is beyond the confines of this current life is that his reliance on traditional beliefs prohibits him from knowing the truth. ("My glory is mine, said the Lord; and I will not give it to another.")

In all honesty, beliefs, regardless of how plausible they may sound, change nothing. Truth changes everything. ("When the Spirit of truth has come, he shall take of mine and show it to you. He shall teach you all things and bring to your remembrance all that I have said.") Those who glory in abstract religious practices glory in self-delusion. They are subservient, bowing to the entities of darkness. ("Behold, Satan has transformed himself into an angel of light.")

Referring to the perversion of truth in Israel's religious customs, the book of Hebrews relates, "And they all having received a good report, *the witness of the law and the prophets,* through faith, received not the promise, *received not the promised reality of the Father's indwelling presence.* God having provided some better thing for us, *the glorified testimony of Jesus Christ,* that they without us should not be made perfect." As Jesus told the Jews, "I speak that which I have seen with my Father, *in the Spiritual world,* and you do that which you have seen with your father, *in the temporal world.*" Regrettably, all of the world's great religions have succumbed to pseudo-spiritual deception. It is not surprising then that Jesus reprimanded the Hebrew priesthood saying, "You fail to enter the kingdom of God yourselves and prevent those who would enter therein."

For certain, that inimitable sensibility we experience as glory is inherent in all men. All have felt the exhilaration that accompanies glory. Likewise, when the soul beholds the brilliance of God's Spiritual glory, it exalts in the magnificence of his light. Awed by its scope and splendor, the prophet exclaimed, "Holy, holy, holy, is the Lord of hosts! Heaven and earth are full of his glory." Jesus referred to the countless manifestations of glory that God had prepared for those who love him, when he said, "In my Father's house are many mansions. If it were not so I would have told you." Unfortunately, those mansions are too often set upon rocky slopes that no man can climb. They remain there uninhabited, ghosts of our far-off fairer dreams, until we awaken and see their reflections within ourselves. Then, with the first light of that everlasting dawn, we arise and enter into their glory.

A measure of the Spiritual glory infused into the Creator's work is illustrated in the following verse:

Autumn, Son of the Summer Sun, how often I have seen your seed languishing on the granary floor.

Yet you are tomorrow's unbaked bread, the Staff of Life for tomorrow's ten thousands.

The true light that dwells in the midst of Life's "Secret Garden" speaks of the glory granted to man by his Creator. Upon ascending into that eternal light, we are ushered into the Father's radiant presence. Therein, the kingdom prepared for the Son of man from the foundation of the world descends from on high and God's veiled face is made known. The book of Revelation compares this transcending glory to a throne set in heaven. Christ further relates to that analogy, promising, "To him that overcomes I will grant to sit with me in my throne, *in my glory*, even as I also overcame and am set down with my Father in his throne, *in his glory.*" Alluding to the Word's second reading, John's Book of Revelation then discloses, "The throne of God, *the glory of God,* and of his Christ shall be revealed there. They shall see his face and his name, *his knowledge,* shall be written in their foreheads."

As indicated in the preceding translations, when Christ asked the Father to glorify his Son with his own Spirit and God replied, "I have glorified you; and I will glorify you again," two distinct forms of glory were brought to light. To understand what these two glories signify we must first recognize what Spiritual glorification implies. Simply stated, glorification is the imparting of Life to any form that replicates God's Spirit. Therefore, when the Father outpictured his quickening principles into Creation, he imparted his glory to all that he had made, for all that appeared characterized his Spirit.

Scripture identifies the glory that emanates from the midst of created form as the Christ, "who is the brightness of the Father's glory and the express image of his person." Both the Son of man and Christ, *which are one and the same,* were glorified with this inherent glory. The first glorification was accomplished through the externalizing of God's signs and wonders. ("Behold, I set my bow *my Spiritual similes,* in the cloud.") The second glorification was accomplished through the internalizing of God's signs and wonders. ("Father, glorify your Son with your own Self.") Therein, the Son of man is glorified through recognition of God's external glory, and Christ is glorified through recognition of God's internal glory. ("I have glorified you and I will glorify you again.") As Jesus explained to his disciples, "You shall go in and out and find pasture."

As a foreshadowing of this second glorification, God's revelatory signs and wonders appeared as principled analogies that characterized his Spirit. ("My Father works hitherto and I work also.") Until the two aspects of this revelatory work were finished, the Word-body of Christ could not receive a second glorification. But, after the Creator's signs and wonders were Spiritually embodied and demonstrated in Christ, a second glorification quickly followed. ("If God is glorified in the Son, he shall glorify the Son in himself; and he shall straightway glorify him.") Thereafter, Christ's first glory, *his pseudo-spiritual glory,* and his second glory, *his Spiritual glory,* were both imparted to man. Thus, upon receiving this second witness, *the Word's "second resurrection,"* man's preordained heritage was fulfilled. Recognizably, this second manifestation of the Son of man's glory accounts for Christianity's belief in Christ's "Second-Coming."

The following verse speaks of the everlasting glory that God imparts to man at Christ's appearing:

All the works of God express his glory. He has shaped the spheres and filled the void with their resonant songs.

The day declares their splendor; and the night gives way to their voice. He directs their movements and orchestrates the ebb and flow of their harmonious accords.

His glory extends from the one end of heaven to the other. There is no place where his song is not heard.

Come, let us rejoice in its unbroken melody; let us enter into the Lord's everlasting glory.

In keeping with the Creator's two instructional works, Scripture's account of Christ's first glory, *his pseudo-spiritual glory,* begins with the book of Genesis and ends with his crucifixion at Golgotha. An account of his second glory, *his Spiritual glory,* commences with his resurrection and continues through the book of Revelation. Notwithstanding, the entire Bible offers a first and second reading of Christ's presence. Its message can therefore be translated either externally, *the Word's first reading,* or internally, *the Word's second reading.* It is, at once, both pseudo-spiritual and Spiritual. As Paul witnessed, "The Father has translated us, *his pseudo-spiritual Word,* into the kingdom of his beloved Son, *his Spiritual Word.*"

Identifying these two forms of glory in man leads to the discovery that there are also two forms of eternal rest available. The first rest is noted in the book of Genesis when we are told that God completed his work in six days and on the seventh day he rested from all that he had created and made. A second rest was indicated when Jesus came preaching the kingdom of God saying, "Come unto me, you that are weary and heavy laden, and I will give you rest." A second rest is also given credence when

Christ says, "My Father works hitherto and I work also." The question is thus raised, "How could God rest and continue to work at the same time?"

We should not be confused by what appears to be conflicting testimony, for God's rest and Christ's rest are complementary. ("All that the Father has are mine.") When God entered into his rest, he entered into Creation's glory; and when Christ entered into his rest, he entered into God's glory within Creation. Both rests are thus recognized as extensions of the Creator's Person. Just as the Father rested in the glory of his completed work, so was the Son to rest in the glory of his completed work. ("Father, I have finished the work that you gave me to do. Now I come to you.") In the same context, man was to rest in God's glory at the completion of his Spiritual work. As the book of Revelation relates, "They shall rest from their labors and their works do follow them."

Therefore, upon entering into Christ's rest, we are glorified with the knowledge and glory that was extended to him from the foundation of the world. Through Christ's glorification, the works of the law and the prophets thus found rest in mankind. They evolved from a system of pseudo-spiritual will-worship into the true light of that Spiritual rest that previously lay hidden from man's eyes. ("In that day I shall call them my people that were not my people, and my beloved who was not loved.")

The relationship existing between God's rest and his glory is further clarified in the following comparisons:

- "His rest shall be glorious."
- "The Lord said, This is the rest, *the glory,* wherein I will cause the weary to rest, *to glory,* and this is the refreshing wherein they shall be refreshed."
- "Let us therefore fear, lest a promise having been left to us of entering into his rest, *of entering into his glory,* any of us should fall short of it."

- ■ "For those who sincerely believe on Christ do enter into his rest, *do enter into his glory.*"
- ■ "There remains a rest, *a glory,* for the people of God; and he that has entered into his rest, *his glory,* has ceased from his own works."
- ■ "The Lord has said, In returning and rest, *in returning to my glory,* shall you be saved. In quietness and confidence shall be your strength."

When we speak of what is saved and what is lost on earth, we should understand that what is saved is the Spiritual glory that was imparted to man from the foundation of the world. What is lost is man's departure from that glory. As Scripture relates, "If any man would glory, said the Lord, let him glory in this: That he knows me," *that he has entered into my glory.*

Assenting to the all-encompassing glory that emanates from within the Creator's work, the psalmist presents the following analogy:

"The heavens, *the greater lights,* declare the glory of God; and the firmament, *the lesser lights,* shows forth his handiwork. There is no speech or language where their voice is not heard.

Their line, *their glory,* has gone out through all the earth, and their words, *their truths,* to the end of the world. In them he has set a tabernacle for the Sun, *a tabernacle for the Son.*

There is nothing hid from the heat, *the fiery truth,* of it. The principles of the Lord are perfect, converting the soul. Their testimony is sure, making wise the simple."

There is no adequate way of conveying the sublime affect that God's glory has upon the soul. His true light speaks, but not of itself. It responds when man cries out to his Redeemer for deliverance; and it listens, searching out the heights and depths of the heart. It gives Life to the lifeless and beauty in exchange for ashes. Indeed, the glory of the Lord is man's exceeding great reward ("I am your exceeding great reward."), giving payment in kind for the soul's return to him who gave it.

Therefore, in giving, we experience the glory of giving. In loving, we experience the glory of loving. And in glorifying God within ourselves, we experience the radiant glory of his everlasting presence. As the children of God, we are raised up by the glory that is in us, and as the Sons of God we are passed from glory unto glory. All is performed according to the glory of the Lord.

9

I Am the Life

"And he showed me a pure river of water of life, clear as crystal, proceeding out of the throne of God and of his Christ.

In the midst of the street of it, and on either side of it, was the Tree of Life; and the leaves of the tree were for the healing of the nations."

REVELATIONS 22:1-2

If ten different people were asked to define "life," we would probably receive ten different replies. Generally, the word "life" is used so loosely, it could allude to almost anything. Still, for our immediate study, we will consider only two of life's features; namely, Life as the Source of all power and life as the consequence of all power.

When I first began studying life in-depth I was confronted with the problem of how to correlate dissimilar substances, the tangible and the intangible. My initial success in probing intangible substances was extremely limited. At times I questioned whether it was possible to understand their Spiritual configurations, but my perseverance and sincerity were eventually rewarded. As I continued my studies, evidence mounted disclosing that tangible Creation was replicating the intangible Life that supported its myriad forms. All adhered to the reproductive law of bringing forth after its own kind. This led to the conclusion that external life, in its entirety, was a Spiritual parallelism. What visibly appeared was nothing less than an expression of things not seen. I then realized that probing into the unknown called for a complete reappraisal of my previous beliefs.

I am confounded at how easily the mind overlooks the obvious. In retrospect, I should have recognized that the psyche was the most logical place to begin my search into life's mysteries, for thought belongs to that invisible realm wherein all things visible are conceived. It took almost five years of study to arrive at that simple truth, which is a relatively short time considering mankind has been pondering life's mysteries for thousands of years. Thereafter, I set myself to the task of restructuring my previous knowledge, of reconciling the intangible within Creation to the intangible within myself. ("Through study and deliberation we understand that things are not made by those things which do appear.")

As my knowledge relating to the intangible increased, it became clear that Creation's common denominator was the light of Life embodied within all living things. The evidence was overwhelming. What applied to Creation also applied to God and man:

- All proceeded from an intelligent Source.
- All emanated from a Principal having Life within itself.
- All created form was a reflection, or a personalizing of that quickening force we call God.

Bringing forth after its own kind, the God-Principal had given tangible birth to its intangible Spirit. The true light that radiated from the midst of visible manifestation was characterizing its quickening Source. The light expressed the Life and the

light was the Life. ("In him was Life and the Life was the light.")
Currently, we have recognized the light of Life as the Christ, the
first begotten of the Father. Scripture speaks of the radiant light
of Christ's presence within Creation as he that dwells in the
midst of the Garden of God. ("The Lord walked in the midst of
the Garden.") Just as the mind's knowledge was an invisible entity
in the midst of human form, so Christ's knowledge was an
invisible entity in the midst of Creation's form. The mysteries
surrounding heaven and earth thus came to rest upon man and
the Son of man. ("Darkness shall cover the earth, and gross
darkness the people; but upon him, *Christ's Spiritual character,*
has the light shined.") Through an inversion of Christ's concilia-
tory efforts, I finally understood the principle of one all-inclusive
God and, thereafter, I recognized that all form was an expression
of his eternal glory. ("There is none other besides me, said the
Lord. Whatsoever is under the whole heaven is mine.")

The notable difference between the structuring of man and
the structuring of Creation is that in preparing the Universe,
intangible intelligence was translated into tangible form. However,
in man, that process was reversed; tangible form was translated
into intangible intelligence. What initially came out from the
Father now returned to the Father. ("I came out from the Father,
now I return to the Father.") Visible Creation thus served as a
bridge of passover between two intelligent entities; namely, the
true light within Creation and the true light within man.

Upon recognizing this reversal in Creation's flow, my efforts
to correlate the visible world of substance to the invisible worlds
of God intensified. All the while, evidence mounted showing that
these three, God, Christ, and man, agreed in One.

Of the many things to be learned about life is that all of
God's work is in motion. All is in a state of flux. All is either
evolving outward or inward. ("You shall go in and out and find
pasture.") In the external world, evolution is at work. In the

internal world, involution is at work. Primarily, man was designed for involution: to evolve within the intangible parameters of God's work. His role was, therefore, one of transition. He was not to be an end in himself. Like his Creator, he would be a work in progress, a work that would continue into infinity.

With the advent of involution, God breathed the Spirit of Life into Adam and man became a living soul, *the living Life.* But, adhering to the reproductive principle that everything was to bring forth after its own kind, man inherited the dark conditions experienced by God when he emerged from the void. Just as the Creator had given Life to the attributes of darkness that were present at his inception, man now gave life to the attributes of darkness that were present at his inception. With the passing of God's work from evolution to involution, Creation's reverse flow in man caused external appearance to serve as outer darkness, and the light of Life within Creation to serve as God's veiled true light. To obtain salvation, man would now need to resolve the differences that divided Creation's tangible darkness from God's veiled intangible light.

Creation's darkened tangible form thus became the source of Adam's first knowledge, and Christ's radiant light within tangible form was externally darkened, reappearing within man as pseudo-spiritual knowledge. Consequently, the true light in all that God had made was consigned to darkness. ("He was in the world, and the world was made by him, and the world knew him not.") The visible and invisible worlds of the mind, the visible and invisible worlds of Creation, and the visible and invisible worlds of God's Spirit thus emerged in darkened accord. All reflected the Creator's primal condition when he emerged from the dark abyss. The light of Life was obscured by darkness, and the darkness within mankind recognized it not. ("He made darkness his pavilion.")

This sharing of visible and invisible attributes by God, Christ and man further reflects their all-inclusive unity. How man shares in this threefold equation is seen in the following:

- He is the Life. Made in the image and likeness of God, he is *by extension* empowered with the Creator's quickening ability.
- He is a quickening Spirit. Made in the image and likeness of God, he has power to give Life to the lifeless, to raise temporal form from the death of external darkness, and to provide it with the light of Life.
- He is the light of Life. Made in the image and likeness of God, he is the light of Life that was first personalized in Adam, and he is the light of Life that was later personalized as Christ. He is the Alpha and Omega in microcosm; the beginning and the end; the First and the Last."

In achieving this unity, man enters into his higher calling and fulfills his Spiritual heritage. ("We who were without knowledge of eternal truth has he quickened together to sit in heavenly places with Christ.")

One of the questions most frequently asked, and generally left unresolved, is this: If man was created in God's image and likeness, why is he limited to creating inanimate objects? This, of course, excludes giving life to his children and providing the light of Life for knowledge quickened within himself. The reason for his inability to impart Life to material objects becomes clear once we understand that man was designed primarily for involution, not for evolution. When he uses the faculties fashioned for involution to further evolution, he circumvents the eternal pattern. What he shapes with his own hands returns to the dust out of which it was formed. His labors, therefore, culminate in death. In keeping with the Creator's primal directive, everything must bring forth after its own kind. Man's work is no exception. He that sows the light of Life reaps *the Spiritual* light of Life, and he that sows the darkness of death reaps *the pseudo-spiritual* darkness of death.

It is a paradox that man should be made in the image and likeness of God and fail to understand his relationship to the Creator. Accounting for this limitation, the disciple John explained, "No man has ever seen the Father. The only begotten, *the light of Life,* which is in the bosom of the Father, he has declared him." Therefore, to know God, we must look to the inherent true light that resides within his work and witnesses to his all-inclusive unity.

Once we begin communicating with God in Spirit and in truth, the reciprocal principles that characterize his presence are clearly recognized. Consider the following:

- Life is Spiritually recognized as a mutually shared relationship. ("I am in the Father and the Father is in me. He that has seen me has seen the Father.")
- Life is Spiritually recognized as a mutually shared, all-encompassing state. ("All things were made by him and without him was not anything made that was made.")
- Life is Spiritually recognized as a mutually shared, all-encompassing characterization. ("The Word was with God, and the Word was God; and the Word was made flesh.")
- Life is Spiritually recognized as a mutually shared, all-encompassing energy Source. ("As the Father has Life in himself, so has he given to the Son to have Life in himself.")
- Life is Spiritually recognized as a mutually shared, all-encompassing parallelism. ("I do only those things which I see with the Father.")

We thus see the light of Life that came out from God characterizing the light of Life that abides in God. This same revelatory light appears in man as a summation of those eternal truths that abide within the Father.

When the book of Revelation discloses, "They shall see his face and his name shall be written in their foreheads," it indicates that God's face is conveyed to us through the knowledge embodied in his inherent principles. As the psalmist writes, "Cause your face to shine upon us, O Lord, and we shall be saved." We thus understand that God's face, *the principles wherein Life is quickened,* can be seen only through his paralleling light. Sequentially then, the light of Life that provides mankind with Spiritual knowledge mirrors the light of Life that emanates from within Creation, and the light of Life that emanates from within Creation mirrors the light of Life embodied within the Creator's witnessing principles. We thus see the principles that emerged with God and his light at their primordial inception imparted to all that was thereafter made. ("His line has gone out throughout the whole earth.") And, because man was framed as a mirrored extension of all that preceded him, his face, *like that of the founding principles imparted to him,* appears in all faces. ("The Father and I are one.")

10

I Am the Way

"Behold, I do a new thing, said the Lord. I will make a way in the wilderness and cause rivers to flow in the desert.

My people shall drink from its streams and those whom I have formed for myself shall show forth my praise."

ISAIAH 43:19-21

With the creating of Adam's sensory body, tangible Creation was translated into intangible thought. But when Adam failed to relate to the light that radiated within himself and from Creation's midst, his thoughts succumbed to darkness and death. Therein, they became Lifeless entities, *entities incapable of "knowing God."* Perceiving the elements of light and darkness as good and evil ("The Tree of Knowledge of good and evil") he was forced to exit Eden, *to forfeit the true light that related him to God's work.* The thoughts of Adam and Eve were thus consigned to outer darkness. There, they began toiling in the dark realms of an externalized world. ("I have cursed the ground for your sake. In sorrow shall you eat of it all the days of your life; thorns and thistles shall it bring forth to you; and throughout your days you shall eat bread in the sweat of your face.") To bring an end to the dark days of his earthy pilgrimage, man would now need to eat of the Tree of Life, *the light of Life,* in the midst of the Garden, *in the midst of Creation.* Only then would his thoughts evolve into God's true light and live forever.

With Adam's failure to conform to Creation's true light and his subsequent exodus from Eden, all knowledge pertaining to the Tree of Life was lost. Isolated from beholding the Creator's Spiritual presence, his temporal thoughts lapsed into somnolence to await redemptive instruction. To provide for that need, God created pseudo-spiritual signs and wonders to light his path and to disclose the Way that would lead to his redemption. ("Your Word, O Lord, is a light unto my path, a lamp unto my feet.") However, due to Adam's darkened state of mind, it was necessary for God to begin his regenerative work at Adam's temporal level of comprehension. The threefold manifestation embodied in the Creator's signs and wonders was thus subject to temporal interpretation. Countless generations would pass before the principles of light witnessed by those similes would lead to mankind's Spiritual reconciliation and redemption. ("He became like me, that I might become like him.") The Spiritual interaction that attended those regenerative similes is witnessed in the following:

- "The Lord bowed the heavens and came down; he descended, and darkness was under his feet."
- "He made darkness his pavilion: he hid in dark waters and covered himself with thick clouds of the skies; and their covering became his secret place."
- "I will go before you and make the crooked places straight. I will give you the treasures of darkness, and the hidden riches of secret places; and you shall know that I am the Lord."

■ "I will bring the blind by a way that they knew not; I will lead them in paths they have not known. I will make darkness light before them, and the crooked places straight."

The Creator thus came to mankind clothed in external signs and wonders, in dark symbolic forms designed to instruct and awaken the mind to its true heritage. Those same dark patterns remain with us to this day, faithfully providing the mind with pseudo-spiritual instruction, *as recounted in the Word's first reading.* In keeping with the three-dimensional nature of God's revelatory Word, Scripture's first reading provides an account of man's ignoble journey into darkness, a journey that presently spans some six thousand years. It is a symbolic portrayal of the degrading way in which his journey began, the meandering path his generations followed as they groped their way through a wilderness of desolate misconceptions, and the glorious way through which they finally discovered and came face to face with Eden's Tree of Life. We should keep in mind that while Scripture is using timeline similes to present these events, the Word of God is nonetheless an eternal parallelism. Its symbolism applies to all generations.

To understand the principle of God's light shining out of mankind's darkness, we must be aware of how the inverse flow of the body's sensory systems affected the mind, for without that inversion of consciousness, man could not have beheld the Creator's glory. The key to knowing God thus lay hidden in man's latent ability to look inward and to recognize himself as a simile of the darkened signs and wonders imparted to him for Spiritual instruction. In that exchange, the psyche's flow of knowledge would be changed from one of external judgment to one of internal judgment, and God would be recognized as all in all. With that accomplished, man would be passed from the death of darkness into the light of Life. Using the body's sensory

faculties to reverse the flow of his work thus became God's intro-
ductory way of overcoming darkness.

The principle of light residing in darkness and then emerging from darkness thus became the cornerstone of God's progressive effort to reconcile his work. ("The stone that the
builders refused has become the headstone of the corner.") That
phenomenon appears in the following:

- When God outpictured his Spirit into Creation, the light that
  emerged from darkness was made to shine in darkness. But
  when the flow of his work was reversed, his light, *through reconciliation,* was made to shine out of darkness.
- When God saw the light of his Spirit radiating from the
  midst of Creation, it appeared as a light shining in a dark
  place. But when the flow of his work was reversed, his light
  was made to shine out of darkness.
- When God formed the first man, Adam, to personify his work
  in microcosm, his light within man inherited darkness. But
  when the flow of his work was reversed, his light, *reappearing as
  the enlightened Son of man,* was made to shine out of darkness.
- When God made his pseudo-spiritual signs and wonders to
  mirror the light of Life embodied in mankind, his light was
  initially made to shine in darkness. But when the flow of his
  work was reversed, *the Son of man was quickened* and his light
  was made to shine out of darkness.
- Before God's signs and wonders were quickened, his light
  within the psyche was made to shine in darkness. But when
  the flow of his work within the psyche was reversed, his light
  was made to shine out of darkness.
- When the flow of God's work was reversed, the Son of man
  was Spiritually glorified and the light that had shown in
  darkness from the foundation of the world was made to
  shine out of darkness.

These examples clearly indicate that God's purpose in providing Creation with an inverse flow was his way of providing the light within his work with the attribute of Self-discovery. By reconciling the internal and external content of his work, he imparted Life to the glory within his light, he imparted Life to his glory within Creation, and he imparted Life to his glory within Man. In all, he caused his light to shine out of darkness.

When the psalmist recognized that the light of Life within Creation was revealed through the Creator's dark similes, he exclaimed:

"Lord, where shall I go and not find your Spirit? How shall I not dwell in your presence?

If I ascend into heaven, you are there; and if I make my bed in darkness, you are there.

When I say, Darkness shall cover me; even the night provides light for me.

The darkness cannot obscure God's presence. Before him, the night shines as the day. The darkness and the light are both alike before him."

From the beginning of time, mankind has failed to understand that all external manifestation carried the mark of God's experience when he emerged from the dark void, that both darkness and light were incorporated into the Creator's character. Paul sought to explain this phenomenon when he wrote:

"We look not to *the deceptive appearance* of things which are seen, but to those things which are not seen. For what we see is temporal; but those Spiritual things that are not seen are eternal.

> In this, we know that if our earthly house were dissolved,
> we have a building of God; a house not made with hands,
> eternal in the heavens."

Regarding this invisible house eternal that appears within created form, let me reiterate that the Christ, *the light of Life,* that first appeared within the Creator's work is the same Christ that gives the light of reality to all generations. ("This is the true light that lights every man coming into the world.") Therefore, when Christ said, "I am the Way, the Truth, and the Life," he disclosed his unseen presence in the continuous whole of God's work. Indeed, he witnessed to God's way and renounced mankind's traditional practices.

Based upon eternal principles, all of God's work begins in darkness. It is his way. It is Creation's way. It is Christ's way. It is man's way. When Jesus said, "I am the Way," he disclosed that he was not only the way of God's external evolution, but, as an extension of the Son of man, had assumed the task of providing God's work with involution. Indeed, the time had come for man to emerge from the dark misconceptions imposed upon his mind and to embrace his preordained role in the heavens. ("I have previously spoken to you in proverbs; but the time is at hand when I shall no longer speak to you in proverbs but I shall show you plainly of the Father.")

Without regard to the restructuring of God's work in Christ and Man, *their passing from temporal evolution to Spiritual involution,* misconceptions relating to Christ's promised return and Scriptures predicted "end of the world" still abound. To correct those errors in interpretation, we should understand the following:

Historically, Creation's outward flow began with God's command, "Let there be light." Its inward flow began with the command, "Let us make man in our image and after our likeness."

The structuring of this inward flow began with the inception of primordial man and reached completion with Christ's last words on the cross, "It is finished!"

Reflecting the timeline that accompanied this endeavor, Creation's inverse flow followed the primordial pattern, beginning with an outflow of pseudo-spiritual signs and wonders. An end to those instructional patterns was signaled when Christ declared, "Now I am no more in the world." Thereafter, the externalizing of God's signs and wonders ceased.

The world now stood on the threshold of receiving a completely new concept of God and his work. Upon entering into this new Age, all life would be perceived as eternal. The Creator's glory would be known through invisible manifestation, even as it was known in visible manifestation. The term, "end of the world," thus signified the completion of God's effort to unite the two aspects of his work and bring them to perfection. ("Be therefore perfect; even as your Father in heaven is perfect.") It did not imply that God intended to destroy his own work. ("What God has joined together, let no man put asunder.")

Why man fails to comprehend his role in God's labors is a mystery. His mind seems fatally obsessed with divorcing itself from Spiritual reality. ("They hated me without a cause.") Jesus referred to this character defect when he told the Jews, "Moses gave you divorcement because of the hardness of your hearts," *a simile of mankind's divorcement from the true light that dwells within his midst.* Following the errors of arbitrary reason, humanity presently awaits the arrival of the kingdom of God on earth; refusing to accept the truth that God's promised kingdom is immediately available. As Jesus assured his disciples, "You shall not have gone through the cities of Judea before the Son of man has come in his Father's kingdom." The Dead Sea Scrolls say it well: "When you shall be two in one body, ('I am in the Father and the Father is in me') then you shall know the kingdom of heaven." Nonetheless, man still insists on digging in the dust of the earth to find answers he should be discovering within himself.

There is a story told that when Christ ascended into heaven's cloud, the angels that received him up looked down upon the faces of his disciples. And the angels asked, "Are your followers prepared for what they must do?" To which Christ replied, "I have given them all that I received from my Father." And the angels persisted, "But what if they fail?" He then looked down upon his little band and responded, "I have no other plan."

11

I Am the Truth

When Pilate asked Jesus, "What is the truth?" his words reverberated with the frustration experienced by everyone who has searched for Life's elusive secret. Pilate was not unlike the rest of humanity. To him, truth was relative. There was always my truth, your truth and the truth of choice. Every man went his own way and lived by his own truth. When the prophet Isaiah saw man's disloyalty, he lamented, "Judgment is turned away and justice stands afar off. Truth has fallen in the street and equity cannot enter. Without cause, he that knows *God's* Truth and departs from evil becomes prey to the fouler." Corrupted by injustice and division, relative truth thus became a self-serving instrument for those who willingly exploited man's weakness.

In a public court of law, the judge and jury decide between what is reasonable truth and what is unreasonable truth. By assuming that judgmental privilege, the faculty of Reason becomes both judge and jury. On the other hand, a precise definition of truth reveals that when reasonable truth is ethically evaluated, it is most unreasonable. Like the handwriting that appeared on the wall of Nebuchadnezzar's palace, relative truth is weighed in the balance and found wanting. Truth in its unadulterated state stands alone, undaunted, absolute, eternal by inheritance. Truth that is pure belongs to God, and what belongs to God has no place in Reason's arbitrary judgments. ("The prince of this world comes and he has nothing in me.") Man's deliverance from reasonable truth thus depends upon his recognition of things that are Spiritually unreasonable, for what belongs to God is always unreasonable to men.

The opposing currents that divide relative truth from absolute Truth should not confuse us. Clearly, there is more than one form of truth. Relative truth witnesses to the ever-changing conditions of the temporal world. Absolute Truth witnesses to the never-changing conditions of the Spiritual world. Relative truth, like temporal man, is of the earth, earthy. Absolute Truth, like the Son of man, is the Lord from heaven. These two forms of truth are as dissimilar as night and day. For sure, the reality that each truth provides determines the quality of life we enjoy.

An in-depth study of these diverse forms of truth leads to only one conclusion: God has generated two distinct types of manifestation. The first manifestation, *the natural world,* witnesses to the truth that resides in temporal darkness. The second manifestation, *the Spiritual world,* witnesses to the Truth that resides in God's eternal light. It is noteworthy that in the Genesis presentation of Creation, evening always precedes the morning. All of God's work begins with darkness and culminates with light. ("And God divided the light from the darkness; and the light he called day and the darkness he called night.") Following that primordial pattern, man is formed in darkness and afterwards emerges into the light. Significantly, his passage between these two worlds is marked by his conversion from time-related truth to non-time-related Truth. ("And when the voice of the seventh angel is heard, time shall be no longer; as he has declared to his servants the prophets.")

One of the marvels of the Bible is that relative truth and absolute Truth both appear within God's revelatory Word as a single entity. This is possible because Scripture's message is, at once, both linear, *historical,* and a parable, *a parallelism: an historical parallelism.* The first reading of God's Word witnesses to relative truth and is, therefore, pseudo-spiritual. The second reading is held in abeyance until the pseudo-spiritual mind is raised and Spiritualized. Its True message then shines through. Since secular Judaism and Christianity disagree over Scripture's interpretation, it would appear that the numerous divisions found in both sects have succumbed to reasonable truth. ("While there are divisions among you are you not yet carnal and walk as men?") Jesus acknowledged the same when he warned his disciples, "He that eats bread with me has lifted up his heel against me." Nevertheless, the Word's second reading comes to Life after Christ's resurrection, *the Word's resurrection,* and witnesses to the absolute Truth that attends God's work. Thus, through the transposing of Christ's Word-body, the light of Scripture's second reading sheds the darkness of the first reading and its light is made to shine out of the Word's initial darkness. Therein, the reader attains life eternal. Thus, through translation, man accomplishes his promised passover between God's diverse states of reality. ("He has translated us into the kingdom of his beloved Son.")

When Christ came to Israel preaching, "I have come as a light into the world that you should not abide in darkness," he spoke of the reconciling work that God had given him to finish; namely, the work of redeeming the darkened Truth held captive by the pseudo-spiritual mind. ("Think not that I am come to bring peace upon the earth, but a sword.") Just as God, *in exiting from the primal void,* had divided his light from darkness, so was it given to the Son of man, *in exiting from the psyche's voidal concepts,* to divide his light from darkness. Christ's intention was not to compound the dark division that plagued the world, but to reconcile the various aspects of absolute Truth that God had imparted to mankind. ("For God sent not his Son into the world to condemn the world, but that the world through him might be saved.") This reconciling work would not be completed until the seed of Truth that Christ had brought into the world was conceived by the mind and Spiritually quickened. ("For you have need of faith; that after you have done the will of God, *embraced the Spiritual Truth within his signs and wonders,* you might receive the promise.")

The work of the Son of man thus became one of regeneration, of breathing Spiritual Life into the pseudo-spiritual hearts and minds of those who had gone astray. ("I have come to gather, *unto myself,* the lost sheep of Israel that have gone astray.") Therein, he would free the Truth held captive by the pseudo-spiritual mind and cause its glory to sit with the Father in heavenly places. ("I shall open the blind eyes and release the prisoners from prison. And those who sit in darkness I shall bring forth out of the prison house.") Relating to this regenerative ministry, the disciples asked Christ to teach them how to pray. In his response he said, "When you pray, ask the Father to feed you with that bread which comes down from above; that his Truth might be done in you as it is in heaven." In concert with that instruction, Christ told his disciples, "Labor not for the meat, *the reasonable truth,* that perishes but for that meat, *that everlasting Truth,* which endures unto life eternal."

It would be impossible to sincerely reflect upon the Life of Christ without eventually recognizing his person as an outpictured parallelism. Whatever touched his life became comparable to the recorded acts of God. As Jesus acknowledged, "All things must be fulfilled, *in heaven and on earth,* that are spoken of me."

Nowhere does this phenomenon become more apparent than in the Genesis account of God's work on the second day of Creation. Consider the following:

"And God said, Let there be a firmament, *a body of Truth,* in the midst of the waters, *in the midst of the Word of Life,* and let it divide the waters from the waters. *Let it divide what is seen in the below from what is seen in the above.*

And God made the firmament, *the Word's signs and wonders,* and divided the waters, *of pseudo-spiritual understanding,* that were under the firmament from the waters, *of Spiritual understanding,* that were above the firmament.

And God called the firmament, *the two aspects of his work,* Heaven."

This symbolic correlation set the stage for making the "two witnesses" of God known and would later be identified with the regenerative similes used to accomplished mankind's Spiritual fulfillment.

Since Creation's inherent law dictates that everything must bring forth after its own kind, we inevitably find ourselves becoming servants of what we create. Just as God labors to sustain his work, so must man labor to sustain his work. In concert with this inherent law, when man creates temporal truths he characterizes those truths within himself and labors to sustain them. As man progresses, he creates pseudo-spiritual truths and again man characterizes those truths within himself and labors to sustain them. When at length man achieves harmony with God's Spiritual Truth, he adheres to the law of ascendancy, but at this juncture in time something changes. Man inherits all of God's work and ceases from his own works. ("He that enters into

God's rest has ceased from his own labors.") Here, man is not only the recipient of God's Truth but, in every sense of the word, he is God's Truth. Jesus verified this unity when he told his followers, "I am the Truth." In keeping with this reciprocal principle, Jesus explained, "What you bind on earth shall be bound in heaven; and what you release on earth shall be released in heaven." It is therefore given to all men to choose the truth they shall serve. But in making that choice we should understand that, regardless of our choice, we shall never be our own. We will always be servants of that we serve.

Because the conflicting facets of relative truth appear in all of the world's great religions, there is none perfect. ("There is none righteous; no, not one.") All must be purged of the mortal dross that veils man's immortal heritage. Jesus, therefore, explained to his disciples, "Other sheep have I not of this fold. Them, *the pseudo-spiritual,* I must bring also; and there shall be one shepherd and one fold." God's higher Truth, *his Christ,* thus becomes the fiery instrument that purges the mind and brings mankind's darkness to light. ("Whose fan is in his hand, and he shall utterly purge his floor.")

As an outcropping of this purging of relative truth, the doctrine of purgatory has arisen. Here, the mind falsely envisions a fiery state of existence wherein the souls of the dead go to be cleansed of error. Since "all have erred and fallen short of the glory of God," it follows that all souls must go to purgatory before being admitted into God's kingdom. Purgatory thus becomes a prerequisite to entering heaven. Akin to the mythical Dante's Inferno, purgatory is typical of the mind's twisted view of the redemptive process. More accurately, knowing the absolute Truth that resides in Christ purges the soul and is directly responsible for man's redemption. ("I baptize with fire and with the Spirit of Truth.") As the prophet relates, "The Lord said to me, 'Behold, I shake not only the earth but the heavens also, that only those things which cannot be shaken may remain.'" Through this shaking of mind and body, "old things, *old mortal errors,* pass away; all things, *all immortal Truth,* become new." Judgment thus receives its eternal inheritance and God's Truth becomes all in all. ("I am the Truth. No man comes to the Father, except by me.")

Having considered the various aspects of this subject, we should understand that whether we choose to walk in relative truth or pseudo-spiritual truth, or at length to walk in absolute Truth, we shall experience the reality of our choice. ("By their fruits you shall know them.") Because we have inherited God's image and likeness, we find our face mirrored in all truth. ("Let no man glory in men for all things are yours. Whether heights or depths, or things present or things to come, all things are yours; for you are Christ's, *both in his affliction and in his glory,* and Christ is God's.") The only remaining question to be satisfied is, "What truth have we personally chosen to serve?" How we answer will inevitably determine the direction of our continuing journey.

12

The Living Word

"And the Word was made flesh and dwelt among us. And we beheld his glory as the only begotten of the Father, full of grace and truth."

JOHN 1:14

Would you be surprised to know that ninety-five percent of those who read the Bible fail to realize that the word of knowledge gathered from its pages and the Word we know as Jesus Christ are one and the same? It is true. When John wrote, "The Word was made flesh and dwelt among us," the essence of his message was that the Word that comprised the law and the prophets was literally embodied in the person of Jesus Christ. Jesus acknowledged the same when he said, "All of the law and the prophets spoke of me." Presently a humanity estranged from God's light receives the messenger but fails to grasp the point that the message and the messenger are one. Consequently, the message that "The Deliverer" came to deliver, the message that God's Word dwells in man ("This is the true light that lights every man coming into the world.") falls on deaf ears.

The miracle that transforms the Bible's Word into "the Word made flesh in Jesus Christ" loses much of its mystery when we recognize its likeness within ourselves. To illustrate, the words you are presently reading are extensions of the thought that gave them Life. They are the light that was generated within the mind by the Life-Source. They are the light of Life. Sequentially then, when the thought is transposed and formally expressed, it becomes the Word of Life, or the Word of God. The Word is with the thought and the thought is with God. The Word's content thus appears as a formal extension of God. ("The same was in the beginning with God.") Therefore, in personifying God's Word, Jesus said, "The words that I speak are Spirit, and they are Life. Of myself I can do nothing. It is the Father, *the Living Thought*, within me, *within the words that I speak*, that does the work."

In like manner, the witness delivered through Moses, Elijah and all of the prophets originated with God. ("Thus saith the Lord.") All were counseled by his thoughts and all personified his Word. Submitting to this higher authority, they came in the name of the Lord, *in the knowledge of the Lord*. They became God's voice in human form, his living Word. ("Behold, I send my messenger before your face, *through the correlation of Spiritual speech*.") As an expression of this unifying order, Moses, Elijah and Jesus conversed on the Mount of Transfiguration, providing a Spiritual simile of the Word of Life they shared in common. Typical of man's pseudo-spiritual weakness, the three disciples that accompanied Jesus into the mount suggested building three tabernacles in that high place; buildings of mortar and stone which they envisioned as glorifying Moses, Elijah and Jesus. But God spoke to them from within his cloud, saying, "This is my beloved Son, *my Word*, in whom I am well pleased. Hear him."

John refers to the Word's everlasting common-unity with the Father when he writes, "The Word was with God, and the Word was God. The same *principle* was in the beginning with God." John thus makes the point that the Word existed long before it was revealed in the Word-body of Jesus Christ. From a genetic standpoint, the Word was first made flesh in man when Adam was formed in God's image and after his likeness. As God's living Word, Adam became Creation's voice, the voice of all that the Creator had made. Since man failed to understand his Spiritual lineage, what the Bible historically records, *from Adam to the days of Jesus Christ,* represents a concerted effort on God's part to restore man's lost heritage, *the Word's lost heritage.* ("I have come to seek and to save that which was lost.") As a participant in that effort, Jesus told his disciples, "Other men have labored, *as witnessed by the law and the prophets,* and you are entered into their labors." However, misconceptions were infused into those Spiritual parameters and understanding of mankind's relationship to the continuous whole was lost. ("You have daubed my house with untempered mortar.")

In keeping with the Word's ongoing redemptive effort, when Moses and the prophets realized their true relationship to God, the psyche was awakened and the pseudo-spiritual mind gave birth to its Spiritual counterpart, "the Son of man." ("You must be born again or you cannot see the kingdom of God.") Isaiah witnessed to this rebirth of the mind into the Son of man as follows:

"Unto us a child is born, unto us a Son is given; and the government shall be upon his shoulders.

He shall be called Wonderful, Counselor, The Mighty God, The everlasting Father, The Prince of Peace.

He shall order his kingdom with judgment and justice; and of the increase of his government and his peace there shall be no end."

In concert with this principle of rebirth, when Jesus asked his disciples, "Who do men say that I, the Son of man, am?" Peter replied, "You are the Christ, the Son of the living God." *You are God's true light in man.* ("Let us make man in our image and after our likeness.") Jesus then acknowledged this truth saying, "Man has not revealed this to you, Peter, but my Father in heaven."

One of the marvels of God's Word is that it brings to light, and judges, all that exists in heaven and earth. ("There is no place that his Spirit is not found.") In that respect the identity of the Word is legion, its measure is from everlasting to everlasting. For example:

- God's Word is like water. It is reflective. "And the Spirit of God moved upon the face of the waters."
- God's Word is like Life-giving rain. It causes the desert to blossom like a rose.
- God's Word is like a river. Its streams are cleansing and refreshing, making glad the hearts of men.
- God's Word is like a wellspring from on high. It brings forth fountains of living water.

These are only a few of the Word's myriad correlations. The Word also has its dark side. That relationship appears in the following:

- God's Word is likened to salt. "But if the salt, *the Word,* has lost its *Spiritual* savor, how shall the earth be salted?"
- God's Word descends from on high as a great deluge, flooding the land *with similes of truth* that create mass destruction and chaos *within the mind.* "As it was in the days of Noah, so shall it be in the days of the Son of man."
- God's Word appears as a great river that overflows its banks, violently uprooting all that stands in its path. "The Word of the Lord is as a destroying storm, as a mighty flooding of waters that overflows its banks."

■ God's Word appears as a wellspring of Life from which the temporal mind may drink. But its thirst will not be satisfied. "He will deprive those *of a temporal mind* who thirst, and make empty the soul of the *pseudo-spiritual* hungry."

Make no mistake, all that God has made has its light and dark sides. It thus follows that mankind, *who is comparable to Scripture's Word,* has his light and dark sides. We should, therefore, understand that the Word's face appears in all faces. That what we see in darkness becomes our darkness and what we see in light becomes our light.

Obviously then, man is a diverse and complex entity. He is not a law unto himself, as many have tried to be. Rather, he is God's living Word, both in Spirit and in truth. All that resides in heaven and earth witnesses to his glory. ("Let all the angels of God witness to him.") Referring to the universal glory imparted to the light-patterns that appear within his Word, the Lord said, "This is the rest, *the light of eternal truth,* wherein the weary shall rest; and this is the refreshing, *the fountain of Life,* wherein they shall be refreshed." Having personalized the Father's promises within himself, Jesus extended the invitation, "Come unto me, *unite with my knowledge,* you who are weary and heavy laden, and I will give you rest."

Until we move beyond the confines of pseudo-spiritual beliefs and will-worship, beyond the confines of doctrinal concepts of an externalized Christ, *who many believe will literally return to earth and establish his Father's kingdom,* the hidden riches of God's Word shall continue to elude us. Jesus revealed what God was, what the Son of man was, and what man was intended to be, when he said, "Father, I have given to them all that you gave to me; that they may be one, even as we are one." Supporting this truth, the apostle warned, "Any spirit that teaches that the Word of God, *the Spirit of truth,* has yet to appear, *or reappear,* in the flesh is not of God." ("To those who look *inwardly* for him shall he appear, a second time, without error unto life eternal.")

Obviously, all is Spirit! All is teeming with Life! The following examples are typical of the countless ways in which God's Word appears as an extension of his light:

- God's Word replicates the light of Life that emerged from the dark abyss. ("In him was Life and the Life was the light.")
- God's Word replicates the light of Life within visible Creation. ("Heaven and earth are full of his glory.")
- God's Word replicates the light of Life after which Adam was fashioned. ("Let us make man in our image and after our likeness.")
- God's Word replicates the light of Life witnessed to man through God's signs and wonders. ("I am your exceeding great reward.")
- God's Word replicates the light of Life witnessed in all of the law and the prophets. ("All of the law and the prophets spoke of me.")
- God's Word replicates the light of Life made flesh in the body of Jesus Christ. ("I am in the Father and the Father is in me. He that has seen me has seen the Father.")
- God's Word replicates the light of Life imparted to man in the Holy Ghost; the eternal truth wherein God and Man become all in all. ("I go unto the Father.")

Regrettably, until now, man has failed to understand that he is God's audible voice within his work. Perhaps we should pose the question to ourselves that Jesus posed to the Jews, "Why do you not hear my words?" Or, maybe we are not yet ready to know ourselves, even as we are known. Perhaps we are more like the false prophet Baal, who looked out over Israel's encampment and prophesied, "I shall behold him, BUT NOT NOW. I shall see him, BUT NOT NIGH." Or maybe we are like the confused disciple who questioned, "Lord, when shall you return and what shall be the sign of your coming?" Has the Spirit of truth been with us so long, and as yet we do not know him? It would appear so.

13

Collective Consciousness

"And Jesus scolded the Jews, saying, You are witnesses
unto yourselves; for you are the children of those who
killed the prophets.

All judgment shall be imputed to this generation;
for the measure of your fathers is fulfilled in you."

MATTHEW 23:31-36

I f you searched for a definition of "consciousness" in the dic-
tionary, it would tell you the word is used to express "the
collective thoughts and feelings of a person or an aggregate
of people." But that explanation is not very informative.
Consciousness is much more than thoughts and feelings. The
Bible sheds additional light on this subject when it speaks of
consciousness as living soul, as the body's living Life.

Since the rudiments of consciousness in man begin with the
body, it is here that we must commence our search for a broader
understanding of what consciousness, or the soul, truly represents. When we analyze the human frame, we quickly discover
that although we perceive ourselves as individually different, all
of humanity is essentially the same. Genetically, man's ethnic
heritage is of no consequence. All races are fashioned from the

same elements, from quickened stardust gathered from the far reaches of the Universe. In essence, we are invisible, the substance of microscopic protons, electrons and neutrons, which have bonded together to create the genes and cells that form our flesh and blood and bone. Although we are not cognizant of the fact, billions of unseen forces daily live and move and have their being within our anatomy. Indeed, we are not our own. "We are fearfully and wonderfully made."

From the midst of this astonishing anatomical mass emerges a combination of miraculous powers and perceptive faculties that provide the nucleus for man's very existence. Collectively, these faculties form a sensory body, which in turn gives birth to sensory consciousness. This assemblage serves as a bridge over which the substance of God's visible world passes to enter his invisible world. Through sensory conversion, external Creation is recast into internal thought and man's living soul emerges as an extension of Creation's Living Soul, *the intelligent Over-soul we call "God."* Fashioned in the same image and likeness, and sharing equally in the Life and elements that sustain all things, these two Souls complement each other as one flesh.

Although the senses are responsible for many of humanity's difficulties and misdeeds, evidence shows that without their inverse capability, man could not know God; for through sensory activity, Creation's flow is changed from evolution to involution and all returns to its Source. Therein, all that came out from the Creator returns to the Creator. ("I came out from the Father, now I return to the Father.") We thus determine that the sensory body is an essential link in the Creator's work; that, through sensory conversion, Creation's visible and invisible aspects are transposed into collective thought and perpetuated in man. ("I am the light of the world," *the light of God's glory within Creation.)* The mind's first state of consciousness is thus recognized as a composite of Creation's diverse nature.

In exploring the intricacies of the human frame, we should remember that all thought is based upon quickened symbolism. As previously explained, all knowledge is comprised of word-symbols, all word-symbols are comprised of letter-symbols, and all letter-symbols are quickened by the Life that gives symbolism conscious reality. The mind's correlated knowledge is thus recognized as an intelligent extension of its Life-Source. It is the light of Life. ("I Am that I Am.") The book of Genesis refers to this transposing of structured symbolism into human cognizance when it relates, "And God breathed into man's nostrils the breath of life, and man became a living soul." *He became an extension of that symbolism that witnessed to its Causal Source.* The mind's Collective Consciousness is thus identified as Spiritually ordered imagery, as knowledge quickened and shared by God and man in common.

Since Creation's basic tenet decrees that life is to bring forth after its own kind, we see visible form transposed through the senses and resurfacing within man's faculty of memory as a nebulous entity. In turn, memory brings forth after its own kind, allowing that committed to its keeping to be consciously retrieved as desired. The mind is thus provided with an ever-expanding storehouse of imagery and knowledge, all of which provides a continuing base for man's progressive involution. Since memory depends upon the body's sensory system to lay in store whatever the mind may or may not require, its impressions are essentially of the earth, earthy. ("And Eve took of the fruit of the Tree of Knowledge of good and evil and ate of it . . . and gave it also to Adam.") Accordingly, Eden's Tree of Knowledge, *a metaphor for temporal Creation,* was seeded into the human frame through the mind's faculty of memory.

When we apprise the faculties of imagination and emotion, it becomes painfully clear that man and beast share the unpredictable responses of these two entities. Generally, imagination incites emotion, triggering uncertain results. Those responses can be sublime, beautiful, exhilarating, or in their worse scenario, devastating. Yet these powers have no authority of their own. They respond solely to the faculty of temporal Reason.

Although sensory Reason is commonly associated with judgment, it is void of Spiritual expertise. Therefore, after Reason had enthroned itself within the mind, judgment began appearing in man in two distinct forms. There was temporal judgment and there was Spiritual judgment: a first judgment and a last judgment. There was a judgment based upon Reason and a judgment based upon eternal truth. Since man's initial state of reality is ordered by his sensory system, the faculties of Reason, imagination and emotion formed a devastating trilogy, compounding the dark illusions that from the beginning of time had plagued the Creator's work.

Having briefly considered the sensory mechanism that governs the physical and mental bodies, we can now move forward to review the three branches that comprise the intellectual body. Once again, we are not as individual as first believed. As previously disclosed, there are three intellectual states. The first two are a mixture of temporal and pseudo-spiritual thought and are experienced by man as the pseudo-spiritual mind. The third is Spiritual thought, which is attained when the temporal dross is removed from pseudo-spiritual thought. Jesus confronted these differences when the Jews insisted they were righteous because they were Abraham's seed. Challenging their viewpoint, he replied, "If you were Abraham's seed you would do the works of Abraham." Unlike his protestors, Jesus knew that more than one form of intellectual seed appeared in man. The temporal mind witnessed to things that were temporal, the pseudo-spiritual mind witnessed to things that were pseudo-spiritual, and the Spiritual mind witnessed to things that were Spiritual. The Jews that he addressed evidently knew nothing of these various divisions.

Though Scripture singularizes all of mankind as Adam, it also acknowledges a first and second seed. In that regard, Paul writes, "The first man, Adam, was made a living soul. The second man, Adam, was made a quickening Spirit." Enlarging upon the mind's threefold reality, the apostle explained, "As in the first Adam, *the temporal and pseudo-spiritual minds,* all men die, so in Christ, *the second Adam,* all are made alive." Although the Jews regarded themselves as extensions of Abraham's temporal seed, they clearly failed to identify with the Patriarch's Spiritual understanding of God. They were therefore perplexed when Jesus said, "Before Abraham was, I am. Abraham rejoiced to see my day, *the light of my knowledge,* and when he saw it he was glad." Christ thus introduced the Jews to a previously concealed truth, the living presence of an all-inclusive Collective Consciousness.

The principle of collective thought is easily grasped once we recognize that the only perceptible difference between generations past, present and future is the knowledge acquired along the way. Because consciousness is based upon quickened knowledge, the discoveries of previous generations are assimilated by today's society, providing the mind with its current reality. All generations are thus linked together to form a common "living soul." All live and move and have their being in one progressive consciousness. All are integrated into one solitary Life. ("God is not the God of the dead, but of the living; for all live unto him.")

Thus, in keeping with the principle of reassimilation, *the principle of everything bringing forth after its own kind,* we see the Collective Consciousness of all generations passed from life unto life. Because mankind inherits life's continuous whole, Scripture relates, "The errors of the fathers shall be visited upon the children unto the third and fourth generations." Having recognized that both evolution and involution are based upon the integrating of knowledge and that our knowledge constitutes our identity, we come to the truth that we are the life that has survived the graves of all previous generations. Indeed, we are life after death! ("It is the Spirit that quickens; the flesh profits nothing.")

The book of Hebrews speaks of life's progressive continuity in the following manner:

"And you, Lord, in the beginning laid the foundation of the earth; and the heavens are the works of your hands.

They shall, *in a linear manner,* perish; but you remain. They shall wax old like a garment, and as a vesture you shall fold them up and they shall be changed.

But you are the same and your years shall not fail."

The concept of consciousness belonging to the continuous whole of an evolving Creation introduces us to Christ's promise of entering into life eternal, for thoughts built upon eternal principles are eternal in themselves. Knowledge thus becomes the key to comprehending life eternal, for by clarifying our knowledge, we understand that, as participants in the continuous whole, we reside in a world without end.

Three levels of Collective Consciousness are thus recognized as being available to mankind. The first two levels, *temporal and pseudo-spiritual consciousness,* view life as a succession of terminal states and witness to the mind's error and delusion. The third level, *Spiritual consciousness,* witnesses to the truth and validity of Christ's insights into life eternal. Nonetheless, all levels have their being in the continuous whole. All are passed from life unto life. As the Word corroborates, "He that is unjust, *the temporal mind,* shall continue to be unjust. He that is righteous, *the pseudo-spiritual mind,* shall continue to be righteous. And he that is holy, *the Spiritual mind,* shall continue to be holy." Jesus therefore taught, "Those who do good shall come forth to everlasting righteousness, and those who do evil shall come forth to shame and everlasting contempt."

Those who doubt the concept of Collective Consciousness need only to consider the progression of knowledge that has taken place within this current generation. Have we not all incorporated today's knowledge into our present identity? Doesn't our present state of mind exist as an internal microcosm of life's external progression? Absolutely! When we review events that have taken place throughout the Ages, an undeniable truth comes to light: all is the substance of collective thought. Beyond question, man is a work in progress. What we claim as our own is not our own. It is the product of countless generations. We have only added to its measure and moved their work forward. ("Other men have labored, and you are entered into their labors.")

From the very beginning, when God formed Creation, what emerged was the Collective Consciousness of the Most High; and when he formed Adam in his own image and likeness, man became an extension of the continuous whole. The soul thus emerged in complete unity with its Creator, a replica of that light that was formed before the world was.

The fact that mankind failed to recognize this truth laid the foundation for Christ's promise to raise all generations from the dead. ("And I, if I be lifted up, *if my knowledge is lifted up,* I shall draw all men unto me.") With the fulfilling of Christ's resurrection, the dead in Christ, *those who witnessed to the Word's true light in all generations,* came forth from their graves. We who today keep his Spiritual testimony are likewise caught up with him in the clouds, *in previously clouded testimony.* So shall we ever be with the Lord. In the same context, Christ said, "The hour has come when all who are in the graves shall hear the voice of the Son of man, *the voice of the Spirit of truth,* and those who hear shall live."

This explanation should aid in understanding what Jesus meant when he told the Jews, "You are witnesses unto yourselves; the measure of your fathers is fulfilled in you. Therefore, all judgment shall be required of this generation." Perhaps, after so long a time, Cain's question, "Am I my brother's keeper?" can be answered with a resounding, YES! For we now understand that today, tomorrow and thereafter, others shall harvest, in kind, the seeds we have planted. Indeed, we shall all be there, to reap what we have previously sown. It cannot be otherwise. It is our eternal heritage. ("I have power to lay down my life; and I have power to take it up again.")

14

Christ Consciousness

"And Christ spoke to the Jews, saying, Search the
Scriptures; for in them you think you have eternal life:
and their words testify of me.

But you will not come to me that you might have
life."

JOHN 5:39-40

Having completed our discussions on regeneration and
how knowledge is perpetuated to form the mind's
Collective Consciousness, we are now ready to
explore the subject of Christ Consciousness. The difficulty
encountered in venturing into this realm of study is set forth, in
parable form, when Christ quotes Abraham, *in the Spiritual
afterlife,* as saying, "Though one should return from the dead
and confirm what I have said, they will not be persuaded." The
purpose of these discussions, however, is to impart understanding, not to persuade.

Before exploring the parameters of Christ Consciousness,
which is comparable to life eternal, let me first restate the truth
that all phases of God's work are factored into a common
denominator. All substance exists as a visible expression of God's

Spirit; all is quickened imagery. Accordingly, the seen appears as a replica of the unseen, and therein Creation is recognized as an outpictured facsimile of God's Spiritual character. The parallelism "as above so below" speaks of this alliance and the mind's three stages of progressive development witness to the same.

In agreement with this union, at Creation's inception, God created two of every kind of living thing that moved upon the face of the earth, *reflecting the principle that it takes two witnesses to fulfill the law of Life.* We should, therefore, not be surprised to find that same pattern emerging within the mind. On the terrestrial level, there is temporal consciousness and pseudo-spiritual consciousness. Their characteristics, being comparable, are counted as one flesh. On the Spiritual level, there is God Consciousness and Christ Consciousness; and their characteristics, being comparable, are counted as one Spirit. ("The Father and I are one.") We thus find four types of collective thought available to man — two witnessing to the first man, Adam, and two witnessing to the second man, Christ. Although the patterns formed by each of these are perceptibly different, all find expression in Creation's order; all exist as witnessing imagery.

The evolving of the first two levels of cognizance into Christ Consciousness is expressed in this presentation as entry into parallel thought, or the Word's second reading. This redirecting of the pseudo-spiritual psyche is acknowledged by Jesus when he informs his disciples, "The kingdom of God, *the light of Life,* is within you. The kingdom of heaven, *the light of Life,* is among you." Thus, with Christ's revelation that God's kingdom resided within mankind's midst, a new Age of understanding dawned upon civilization. In concert with this Spiritual awakening, Jesus announced, "The law and the prophets, *the mind's linear understanding of life,* was until John. Now, the kingdom of God, *the mind's parallel understanding of Life,* is preached." With the advent of Christ Consciousness, the mystery kept from the foundation of the world was resolved. The Word-body of Christ would, thereafter, be recognized as a metaphor signifying the mind's entry into a state of eternal comprehension. ("For we have the mind of Christ.")

What mysteriously takes place in man's ascent into Christ Consciousness is the conversion of the Word's pseudo-spiritual testimony, *the Bible's first reading,* into Christ's Spiritual testimony, *the Bible's second reading.* ("No man has ascended into heaven, except he that came down from heaven; even the Son of man which is in heaven.") John's book of Revelation introduces the reader to Christ Consciousness with the narrative:

"The testimony of Jesus Christ, *the Word's personification in the person of Christ,* which God gave to him, to show unto his servants those things that must shortly come to pass, *those things to be Spiritually fulfilled at the Word's second reading."*

In that context, Christ Consciousness immediately begins when the mind adopts the Word's eternal truth. ("For this is life eternal: To know God and Jesus Christ whom he has sent. *To know God and to communicate with him through the true light that he has sent.*")

One of the most difficult tasks in learning something new is the challenge we face in unlearning the old. Any true renewal of the mind must be accompanied by a drastic clarification of all first knowledge. ("In Christ, old things are passed away; all things become new.") For those who experience this transforming of the mind, the unlearning process can be devastating. When the disciples asked Christ about this transitional period he set forth the psyche's conversion in parable form.

Using correlated symbolism, he described man's passover into his promised eternal state as follows:

"Immediately following the tribulation of those days, *in keeping with the relearning that accompanies those days,* the sun shall be darkened and the moon shall not give her light; the stars shall fall from heaven and the powers of the heavens shall be shaken. *This shaking of the heavens is a metaphor that depicts the nullifying of the mind's pseudo-spiritual misconceptions.*

Then shall the sign of the Son of man, *the Spirit of truth,* appear in heaven and all the tribes of the earth, *the mind's temporal thoughts,* shall mourn, *shall suffer loss.* And they shall see the Son of man, *shall experience Christ Consciousness,* coming on the clouds of heaven, *in clouded similes,* with power and great glory.

He shall send forth his angels *of truth* with a great sound of trumpet, *a trumpeting of eternal knowledge,* and they shall gather together his elect from the four winds; from one end of heaven to the other."

To allay the mental tumult of those days, *referred to in the book of Revelation as "the great tribulation,"* the mind's renewal proceeds incrementally. ("He shall feed his flock like a shepherd and gently lead those who are with young.") If it were otherwise, the mind would surely self-destruct.

Personally, I was many years into my studies before I was ready to accept evidence showing that neither heaven nor life eternal lay beyond the grave. In tune with church doctrine, I remained under the illusion that I was here and God's heaven was in some far-off, fairer place. Nonetheless, each time I adopted knowledge pertaining to life eternal being in the present, I discovered anew that Scripture's Paradise was right here on earth. Born of God's Spirit, it was housed in Christ Consciousness. I never cease to be amazed at the ridiculous lengths to which the psyche goes to believe what is untrue and the difficulty it has accepting what is true.

I finally came to the conclusion that if the mind within man and the mind within Christ were of one accord, and if Christ had already ascended into heaven, then the Christ Consciousness that dwelled in man had likewise ascended into heaven. ("We who were dead in trespasses and errors has he quickened together to sit in heavenly places with Christ Jesus.") This was also supported by Christ's disclosure, "I go to prepare a place for you. And if I go to prepare a place for you, I will come again to receive you unto myself, that where I am there you may be also." Other reassuring passages also appeared throughout Scripture.

A much deeper insight into the mystery surrounding Christ Consciousness is obtained once we understand that the seed of this higher reality was sown and conceived through God's signs and wonders. That is, Christ Consciousness was historically embodied in natural form before it was quickened into Spiritual form. ("If I show you earthy things, *if I translate Spiritual knowledge into earthy manifestation,* and you believe me not, how shall you believe if I show you heavenly things?")

This translating of man's pseudo-spiritual state into a higher reality is expressed when John's Revelation compares the forming of Christ Consciousness within man to a woman who is in labor and about to give birth to her new child. Drawing upon the historical experience of the children of Israel, he writes:

"I saw a woman, *the mind,* clothed with the sun, *with God's greater light,* and the moon, *God's lesser light,* under her feet and on her head a crown of twelve stars, *God's judgmental signs and wonders in Israel.*

And she being with child, the *Son of man,* travailed in birth and pained to be delivered; and she brought forth a man-child, *Christ Consciousness,* who was to rule all nations with a rod of iron, the sword of truth.

And the child was caught up to God and to his throne." ("He ascended into heaven and sat down at the right hand of the majesty on high.")

John evidently did not recognize giving birth to Christ Consciousness as an instantaneous or miraculous transition. Conversely, he saw the mind's conversion as historic and incremental. Indeed, the pseudo-spiritual signs and wonders wherein the mind of Christ was conceived, *were assimilated,* over a period of some four thousand years. It began with Adam and Eve in Eden and culminated with Christ's crucifixion and resurrection at Golgotha. With the Son of man's glorification, Scripture's Word in its entirety was quickened and extended to mankind in the Holy Ghost, *the second appearing of God's light within his Word.*

Christ Consciousness is thus identified as a work conceived by God, outpictured by God and fulfilled by God. ("Of myself I can do nothing. It is the Father within me that does the work.") We fall short of understanding the Bible's Spiritual content if we perceive its presentation only as an historical or moral account of man's religious progress. Rather, it is a page-by-page revelation of the Creator's effort to regenerate humanity's first two states of reality and to bring the mind to Spiritual perfection. ("Be therefore perfect; even as your Father in heaven is perfect.")

Then, not unlike the Collective Consciousness that gives life to the temporal and pseudo-spiritual mind, we discover that Christ Consciousness shares in this same all-inclusive unity, for the mind's Ultimate Reality was attained, *and continues to be attained,* through the composite effort of generations that presently span some six thousand years. Therefore, in obtaining the fullness of God's Word, we become the Spiritual fulfillment of those who previously labored to elevate the human soul. We are recipients of the glory they shared with God and made available to us through their testimony. Paul referred to the transcendental aspect of thought when he wrote, "We who are alive and remain shall be caught up with them in the clouds, *in all that was previously veiled,* so shall we ever be with the Lord."

With the labors of those previous generations now brought to fruition, we should understand that until God's revelatory work in the Word-body of the Son of man obtained "a second resurrection," *the resurrection of both mind and body,* the Creator's work remained incomplete. As the Father had used external signs and wonders to glorify the Son of man and to initially introduce Christ Consciousness to mankind, in an inverse manner, he was now using internal signs and wonders to provide Christ Consciousness with a "second quickening," a Self-cognizance that would bring mind and body to Spiritual perfection. ("I have glorified you and I will glorify you again.") All that pertained to God's eternal kingdom was thus internally reconciled and Life's Ultimate Reality became available to all forthcoming generations. ("Eye has not seen nor ear heard, neither has it entered into the hearts of men, the things that God has prepared for those who love him.")

One of the wonders of Christ Consciousness is its inherent ability to reconcile all things unto itself. This is typically recognized when we consider the attributes of Nature's annuals and perennials. The annuals mirror the linear path of the temporal mind, whose seed of life must be planted anew from season to season. This trait is expressed in a linear manner when knowledge is passed from parent to child or from generation to generation.

In these recurring cycles of seeding and rebirth, life's continuity is perceptibly broken and in an illusory manner all appears to culminate in death. Conversely, the perennials reflect the parallel path of Christ Consciousness, whose seed lives on through its root system. Here, life's continuity remains unbroken. Its branches continue to flower and bring forth their fruit in due season, and death is swallowed up with Life.

Clearly, all of God's work witnesses to the truth that the kingdom of heaven, *the consciousness of heaven,* resides in our midst. ("Thy will be done on earth, as it is in heaven.") It challenges us to conform to a new reality, to know that the externalizing of God's revelatory work came to an end with Christ's crucifixion and that all things in heaven and earth have been reconciled. For sure, mankind cannot change Christ Consciousness through systems of pseudo-spiritual will-worship. Rather, Christ Consciousness changes mankind by revealing the Creator's eternal truth. It is we who must convert and be healed. Only then will the "all in all" that God has imparted to his work find peace. ("Then shall I extend to them peace like a river, and their glory shall be as a flowing stream.")

15

The Pseudo-Spiritual Mind

"And Christ said, He that hears my sayings and fails to do them is like a man without a foundation.

Like a man who built his house upon the sand, against which the streams beat vehemently, and it fell; and the ruin of that house was great."

LUKE 6:49

How do you tell the religious zealots of the world, those who pretend to be Spiritual, they are least in the kingdom of heaven? How do you tell the pseudo-spiritual faithful their faith is "without hope, twice dead?" There was a time when I believed the Christian Church aspired to one of the highest callings available to mankind. I was wrong. I was not even close. In fact, all I believed to be Spiritually true was lost in a quagmire of half-truths. As I would later discover, the whole of the religious world was inextricably entangled in a thicket of self-delusion. Paul foretold of the falling away and division that would come amongst those who were misinterpreting Scripture in his day. He warned, "And God shall send them strong delusion that they should believe a lie, because they received not the love of the truth."

Today, traditional religion, as accepted and practiced by the Judeo-Christian community, is an outpictured replica of Eden's Tree of Knowledge of good and evil. As a tree of reasonable judgment, it has two realities: one of good, the other of evil. Swayed by these opposing forces, true Spirituality, *the mind of Christ,* becomes unattainable. ("You make the Word of God of non-effect by your tradition.") Conforming to traditional theology, the worshiper seeks release from the soul's exiled state, all the while misdirected by those he believes capable of leading him to Spiritual freedom. ("Not everyone that says Lord, Lord, shall enter into the kingdom of heaven; but those who do the will of my Father.")

The practice of adopting the half-truths written into religious doctrines is not isolated. Blind acceptance of pseudo-spiritual beliefs under the guise of faith is universal. Like a dark cloud encircling the entire earth, deception and lies engulf all of the world's great religions. Comparable to the disciples of Christ who gathered in the upper room at Passover, each religious sect, convinced of their own righteousness, questions the others as to who the Lord's betrayer might be. All the while, they are confident that the face exposed will not be their own. ("And they asked him, Lord, who is it that will betray you? And he replied, It is he that eats bread with me.")

From Christ's reply we must conclude that all who break bread at his Passover table share responsibility for his death. ("There is none righteous; no, not one.") Paul acknowledged the inclusion of all people in Christ's death when he said, "For as often as you eat of this bread and drink from this cup, *in pseudo-spiritual will-worship,* you show the Lord's death, till he comes." The affect of the deceptive practices imposed upon the Judeo-Christian community is thus seen as both personal and collective, for in adopting their doctrinal distortions, we become servants of the error we serve. We have transgressed God's Word by partaking in traditional will-worship and communion, *a pseudo-spiritual tenet mirroring Christ's betrayal and death.*

Recognizing this, we must now submit to the Spirit of truth embodied in Christ's raised Word-body of knowledge. For therein we share in the likeness of his resurrection. Following the lead of the prophets of old, we must endeavor to make straight within ourselves the path that false doctrines have made crooked. ("Prepare a way for the Lord. Make straight in the desert a highway for our God.")

To be successful in this complex effort, we must first recognize that the reasonable mind is governed by sensory perceptions. Consequently, it views the works of God as linear creation, *as opposed to the Spiritual parallelisms that reveal his true character.* Also, we should be aware that when the psyche is confused, it blindly draws misguided conclusions. ("If the blind lead the blind, shall they both not fall into the ditch?") Convinced of its own authority, the faculty of Reason thus judges truth arbitrarily, imparting its own misconceptions, *its name, its mark, and its number,* on all it encounters. The Book of Revelation portrays that practice as follows:

"And he, *the faculty of sensory Reason,* causes all, both small and great, rich and poor, free and bond, to receive a mark in their right hand or in their forehead, *the mark of sensory cognizance:*

That no man might buy or sell, but he that has the mark, or the name of the beast, or the number of his name.

He that leads into captivity must go into captivity, he that kills with the sword, *the sword of pseudo-spiritual truth,* must be killed with the sword, *the sword of Spiritual truth.* Here is the patience and the faith of the saints."

For sure, the world's religious community is presently over-whelmed by the outpouring of half-truths that are traceable to the faculty of sensory Reason. All doctrines witness to its divisive nature. All bear the conflictive attitude of the temporal mind, *the "mark of the beast."* Indeed, because secular concepts of God and his heaven are so unbelievably diverse, we are counseled to fol-low the religious persuasion of our choice, the one we believe to be most reasonable, the one that best fits our life style.

Although the Jews in the days of the Son of man steadfastly asserted that they were a people under God, when Jesus came preaching unity with God to his countrymen — as opposed to the traditional worship to which they were accustomed — the priestly hierarchy of Israel found his message adversarial, so much so that they plotted his demise. As history records, their fears culminated in his crucifixion and death. Like a curtain about to close upon the final act of a play, the end of Christ's ministry was inevitable. As foretold by the prophets, "They shall look *outwardly* upon him whom they have *inwardly* pierced." They shall ask, "What are these wounds in your hands?" And he shall reply, "These are the wounds that I received in the house of my friends."

The first evidence of the Word's betrayal appeared some four thousand years prior to the events that unfolded at Jerusalem, when God warned Adam and Eve not to eat fruit from the Tree of Knowledge of good and evil or they would surely die. Their disregard for God's counsel led to a state of living death, which became a permanent part of man's heritage. That forewarned death reigned from Adam until Moses, reappeared in the law and the prophets, and culminated with Christ's crucifixion at Golgotha. Thus, all of God's linear work culminated in death. Christ therefore told the Jews, "He that is in error, *he that resides in temporal and pseudo-spiritual thought,* is the servant of error, and the servant abides not in the house forever; but the Son, *the*

Spiritual mind of Christ, abides forever. If the Son shall therefore make you free, you shall be free indeed."

As witnessed by man's history, when the pseudo-spiritual mind falls prey to temporal abstraction, it suffers death. Notwithstanding, once purged of temporal error, man experiences resurrection. ("When Christ had by himself purged our errors he sat down at the right hand of the majesty on high.") Therein, the soul is passed from death unto Life. The Book of Revelation depicts this purging of the mind's reasonable error as follows:

"The beast that you saw, *the mind's reasonable error,* was, and is not; and shall ascend out of the bottomless pit, *that which has no foundation,* and go into perdition.

And they that dwell upon the earth, *those who are given to temporal thought,* shall wonder, whose names were not written in the Book of Life from the foundation of the world, when they behold the beast, *the anomalies of sensory Reason,* that was, and is not, and yet is."

Scripture therefore counts religious orthodoxy as being at odds with God until purged of error. Thereafter, its remaining Truth ascends into heaven. Consequently, the pseudo-spiritual mind is counseled, "Hold fast to that *Spiritual instruction* which you have until I come."

"As Jesus sat with his disciples on a hill overlooking Jerusalem, he turned to his followers and said, See all these things? There shall not be one stone left upon another that is not thrown down."

16

The Stumbling Stone

"Behold, I lay in Zion for a sure foundation a tried stone, a precious corner stone, *but to the pseudo-spiritual mind, a stumbling stone and a rock of offense.* And he that believes in it shall find rest."

ISAIAH 28:16

In the beginning, when the Creator characterized his Spirit in natural Creation, a principle was set in motion that resurfaced when he provided mankind with instructional signs and wonders. However, when the temporal mind was unable to interpret his similes, those enlightening portrayals were made of non-effect. Rather, the mind's temporal error was further compounded. The truth that God's Spirit resided in temporal form was, thereafter, spoken of as "the stone that the builders refused." The blending of this everlasting principle into God's outpictured revelation is expressed in the following passages:

- "He, *the Spirit of the Lord in man,* shall be as a Sanctuary; but for the house of Israel and the inhabitants of Jerusalem, he shall be as a stumbling stone and a rock of offense."

■ "Upon one stone, *the Spiritual light of Life,* shall be seven eyes, *the seven Spirits of God that appear throughout Creation.* I shall engrave the graving thereof; and I shall remove the iniquity, *the dark error,* that plagues that land in one day."

■ "The stone that the builders refused, *the principle of God's living presence within his work,* has become the headstone of the corner."

The children of Israel thus stumbled over translating the out-pictured signs and wonders that appeared within the law and the prophets, and the truth of God's abiding presence within mankind became the stone the builders refused. Nonetheless, the truth embodied in those signs and wonders remained in place, providing a sure foundation for future generations. ("In that day, *the day of the mind's Spiritual enlightenment,* I shall call them my people, who were not my people, and my beloved, who was not loved.") Regrettably, we have only to consider the current divisions that afflict Judeo-Christian doctrine to recognize that God's stumbling stone still causes many to fall. ("Straight is the gate and narrow is the way that leads to Life, and few there be that find it. But wide is the gate and broad is the way that leads to destruction, and many there be that go that way.")

Two types of sanctuary thus became available to mankind. An externalized tabernacle of pseudo-spiritual will-worship that was raised by the faculty of temporal Reason, *which holds promise,* and an internalized tabernacle of Spirit and Truth that is revealed by God, *which fulfills his promise.* The Book of Revelation speaks of this internal sanctuary as follows:

"And the *Spiritual* temple of God was opened in heaven. And the Ark of his testimony, *the Word of Truth,* appeared in his temple. And there were voices, and lightning, and thundering,

and an earthquake, and great hail, *a great shaking of the earth.*
And the angel said, Rise, and measure the temple of God and
the altar, and them that worship therein. But the court that is
without the temple, *the errors of the temporal mind,* leave out
and measure it not; for it is given unto the Gentiles, and they
shall tread the Holy City, *the Word of Truth,* under foot until
the time of the end."

You will note that the opening of the tabernacle of God in
heaven brings with it a shaking out, or purging, of judgment
commonplace to the pseudo-spiritual mind. ("Once more I
shake not only the earth but the heavens also, that only those
things which cannot be shaken may remain.")

With the advent of the Son of man, and the subsequent testimony of the prophets, the promised "foundation stone"
Spiritually materialized within man, indicating the beginning of
a new covenant. The war in heaven thus took a new turn and a
further outpouring of God's pseudo-spiritual signs and wonders
quickly followed. This time, however, his instruction was not
limited to the children of Israel. Rather, it addressed all nations.
With the demise of God's first covenant with Israel, the
Babylonian armies descended upon Jerusalem, pillaging and
burning the holy city and leaving Israel's pseudo-spiritual house
of the Lord desolate. The children of Jacob were carried away
captive into Babylon and their land was left without inhabitants.
From Babylon, they were dispersed amongst the Gentile nations.

The prophet Jeremiah explains the Spiritual aspect of
Jerusalem's desolation when he writes, "For as long as the land,
the mind's pseudo-spiritual sanctuary, lay desolate she kept
S*piritual* Sabbath." The outpictured captivity of the Hebrew people thus signified their reward for corrupting God's revelatory
truth. Subsequently, their pseudo-spiritual inheritance in the

Promised Land was removed from the kingdom of heaven. ("And he that deceived the whole world, *the faculty of pseudo-spiritual Reason,* was cast out of heaven into the earth, and his angels, *his misconceptions,* were cast out with him.")

Christ drew a parallelism between the fate of the Jews and their pseudo-spiritual worship when he said, "When you shall see the abomination that makes desolate, *the replacing of God's authority with pseudo-spiritual Reason,* standing in the holy place, let him that is in Judea flee into the mountains. Let him that is on the house top not come down to take anything out of his house; for then shall be great tribulation." Following that earth-shaking experience, the pseudo-spiritual mind is purged of error and Spiritually redeemed, and the misconceptions of the temporal mind are cast out. ("The one shall be taken, the other shall be left.")

With the advent of God's new covenant, *which coincides with the Word's second reading,* came the Age of prophecy. ("He reveals his secret to his servants the prophets.") For thousands of years, the spirit of prophecy has remained a mystery, but its secret is simply this: The prophets followed God's lead and used external signs and wonders to express Spiritual truth. ("I do those things which I see with the Father.") They recognized God's similes in Israel and their captivity amongst the Gentile nations as a personal parallelism, and they translated the times and events of that Age into Spiritual predictions. ("Behold, the former things have come to pass, and new things I now declare. Before they spring forth I tell you of them.") Therein, visible manifestation was used to represent the mind's trilogy, *its Way, its Truth, and its Life,* and all was abridged into Scripture's Word. ("He has committed all judgment to the Son.")

Israel's downfall through corrupt religious practices is graphically illustrated through the use of symbolism. The need to replace God's first covenant initially appears with David's reference to the Son of man and is further witnessed by Elijah and the prophets. Here are a few examples:

- "My old familiar friend in whom I trusted, *the pseudo-spiritual mind,* He has lifted up his heel against me."
- "Woe to the rebellious children, *the children of tradition,* said the Lord. That take counsel, but not by me; that cover with a covering, but not of my Spirit; that add error unto error."
- "You have trusted in falsehood. Therefore, I will scatter you, *your adulterous ways,* as the stubble that passes away before the wind in the wilderness."
- "I shall lay waste your dwelling places and make desolate your high places. The slain shall fall in the midst of you, and you shall know that I am the Lord."

The apostle Paul speaks of unmasking the transgressions of the pseudo-spiritual mind when he writes, "Then shall that wicked one be discovered; who assuming the authority of God sits himself in the temple of God saying that he is God."

Nevertheless, as the purging of Israel's pseudo-spiritual error progressed, the tenor of the prophets changed. Accusation gradually gave way to the Spirit of Reconciliation:

"Sing, O barren, you that did not bear; break forth into singing and cry aloud, you that did not travail with child; for more are the children of the desolate, *those redeemed from desolation,* than of the married wife, said the Lord.

You shall break forth, *Spiritually,* on the right hand and on the left. Your seed shall inherit the Gentiles and cause the desolate cities to be inhabited.

Fear not, neither be ashamed nor confounded for you shall forget the shame of your youth, *your days of error,* and shall remember the reproach of your widowhood no more; for I am the Lord, your maker and your husband."

Isaiah speaks of the final phase of the mind's reconciliation to God when he writes, "In that day many people shall say, Come, let us go up to the mountain of the Lord, to the house of the God of Jacob. There, he will teach us of his ways and we shall walk in his paths."

Although countless generations have passed since the Age of the prophets and the destruction of Jerusalem, to this day, the stone that the builders refused, *God's Self-revelation in us, the hope of glory,* is rejected. The Spirit of truth patiently stands by, but the promises are still seen as far-off. The pseudo-spiritual mind stumbles and falls and the soul continues its sojourn in an exiled state. The shame and everlasting contempt foretold by Christ therefore remains, and none considers his station in judgment. ("And these all having died in faith received not the promises. But having seen them afar off embraced them, and confessed that they were strangers in a land that was not theirs.")

17

The Captive Exile

"He that leads *the soul* into captivity shall go into captivity; he that kills with the sword *of truth* must be killed with the sword *of truth.*"

REVELATIONS 13:10

When God exiled the children of Israel from the Promised Land, they were carried away into Babylon by the armies of Nebuchadnezzar. There, the Jews became captive exiles, a pseudo-spiritual people dominated by a temporal-minded nation. Nonetheless, submitting his chosen ones to affliction served a dual purpose. It not only chastened them for straying from Spiritual truth, but it also prepared the way for their future redemption. Moreover, as captive exiles, they would now serve as an outpictured example of God's true light shining in darkness. Recognizing the wisdom in this new venture, Isaiah wrote, "The captive exile hastens to fulfill his captivity that he may be loosed; that he should not die in adversity or that his bread should fail." Yet the success of this endeavor hinged upon the mind's ability to translate the true meaning of its captivity into Spiritual enlightenment. ("My strength is made perfect in weakness.")

When the prophets recognized that God's outpictured signs and wonders were Spiritual expressions veiled in temporal form, they concluded from preceding events that the pseudo-spiritual mind had fallen prey to temporal thought, which in turn had led to Israel's captivity. ("What you loose on earth shall be loosed in heaven.") The destruction of the temple at Jerusalem thus served as a warning of what would befall future generations and future houses of worship if they dishonored the Word of the Lord. ("I shall bless them that bless my Word and curse them that curse my Word.") This tenet is restated when Jesus enters the rebuilt temple at Jerusalem and tells the Jews, "Tear down this temple, *the temple of pseudo-spiritual thought,* and in three days, *in Spirit and in truth,* I will raise it up." We must therefore conclude that all traditional forms of worship mirror the attributes of the pseudo-spiritual mind and, regrettably, that the elements of error that alienate the mind from God are present in all churches and synagogues. John therefore writes in his Revelation, "I know the blasphemy of those who say they are Jews and are not, but are the synagogue of Satan." *They are houses of will-worship ruled by the reasonable mind.* The prophet likewise intones, "They shall surely gather together, but not by me, said the Lord."

Directing this truth toward present Judeo-Christian doctrines, we see the circumventing of God's intentions mirrored in today's synagogues and churches. By way of extension, the parallelism formed between the mind and its chosen form of will-worship is reflected in the following:

- The mind's pseudo-spiritual temples of worship "must be born again" or they cannot see the kingdom of heaven.
- The mind's pseudo-spiritual temples of worship "have names that they live and they are dead."
- The mind's pseudo-spiritual temples of worship "claim to see, but they see not. They claim to hear, but they hear not."

And until they convert and become one with the Lord, they
cannot be healed.

■ The mind's pseudo-spiritual temples of worship "look upon
him whom they have pierced," but fail to recognize their own
culpability.

Although these sanctuaries continue to alienate God's Spirit,
they do witness to Scripture's truth. Like the tabernacle that
Moses was instructed to raise in the wilderness of Sinai, their
presence reflects the power, the glory and not least, the forgive-
ness of the Lord. ("Father, forgive them for they know not what
they do.")

Having recognized that the books of Scripture are a revelation
of the Word-body of Christ, and that Judeo-Christian doctrine
reflects the division that has historically plagued God's work, it is
clear that Christ's message continues to be held captive by the
pseudo-spiritual mind. In that captive state, the Word of the
Lord is counted as dead. Both Jew and Christian are therefore
recognized as the dead in Christ. While both embrace the Word's
linear reading, both fail to relate to its parallel truth. By misinterpreting the Word's revelation, the faculty of sensory Reason
has made the promises of God of non-effect. The mind's opposition to eternal truth thus reigns unabated, and the light of
Spiritual resurrection that it seeks is denied. ("All we like sheep
have gone astray. We have turned, every one, to his own way; and
the Lord has laid upon him the inequity of us all.") Therefore,
until such time as the psyche's level of comprehension is
Spiritually raised, its reality is consigned to a state of living death.
("This corrupt must put on incorruption. This mortal must put
on immortality. For the sting of death is error, but the gift of God
is life eternal.")

When we link Judeo-Christian beliefs to Israel in exile, we
find God's rejection of those beliefs voiced throughout the Bible.

As the prophet affirms, "They are a disobedient and gainsaying people who walk in ways that are not good, after their own thoughts." But as God's Spiritual revelation unfolds, provision is made for the deliverance of the mind's captive exiles. As Jeremiah writes, "The Lord has said, When you shall search for me with all your heart, I will be found of you. I will turn away your captivity and gather you from amongst the *temporal minded* nations." ("I will give you power over the nations. As the vessels of a potter are broken into many pieces, so shall they be broken.")

We thus see that God had not left mankind without hope. As the mind's pseudo-spiritual division had contributed to the Word's death, now it would serve as a bridge over which the Word would pass on its journey toward resurrection, ascension and glory. This hidden agenda is confirmed in the following:

- "They that dwell in *pseudo-spiritual* darkness have seen a great S*piritual* light."
- "God has made his S*piritual* light to shine out of *pseudo-spiritual* darkness."
- "He, *the Spiritual Word,* ascended on high and took *pseudo-spiritual* captivity captive."
- "He, *the Spiritual Word,* shall grow up before him as a tender plant and as a root out of a dry *pseudo-spiritual* ground."
- "Though I walk through the valley of the shadow of *pseudo-spiritual* death, I will fear no evil; for you are with me. Your *chastening* rod and your staff *of Life,* they comfort me."
- "You have spread a table *of Spiritual light* before me in the presence of my *temporal-minded* enemies. You have anointed my head with the oil of gladness. My cup is filled and running over."

Because the inverse relationship of darkness to light is fundamental to God's Universe, Paul saw the Word's crucifixion, *the principle of light entering and exiting darkness,* as a necessity. He therefore taught that only by culminating all things in death, *that only by using death to end the power of death,* could salvation be achieved. In that context, he wrote, "We preach Christ crucified. Unto the Jews a stumbling block and unto the Greeks foolishness. But unto those who are called, the power of God and the wisdom of God." Accordingly, the pseudo-spiritual Word in man and the pseudo-spiritual Word in Judeo-Christian worship must suffer death. However, when the Spiritual aspect of the pseudo-spiritual Word is raised from the dead, the Spiritual and the pseudo-spiritual are transposed, *without error,* as one; and their calling in God is fulfilled. ("We who were dead in trespasses and in errors has he quickened together to sit in heavenly places with Christ Jesus.")

Since the temporal mind obtains judgment through the senses, it believes that death occurs when the physical body dies. As repeatedly demonstrated, Scripture refutes that conclusion. Rather, it asserts that all life belongs to God, and in him life is without end. It views life eternal as the mind's raised state of living in The Eternal. ("I am your exceeding great reward.") Conversely, it regards death as living without the knowledge and unity that resides in The Eternal. ("God is not the God of the dead but of the living, for all live unto him.")

So, having been exiled with God's Word in the likeness of his death, we are also raised with him in the likeness of his resurrection. ("The Lord shall descend from heaven with a shout, *with a great thundering of truth,* and the dead in Christ shall rise.") Knowing the end to which all things are predestined, it is expedient that we hasten to end our Spiritual exile. This we can do by conforming to the pattern that was set forth by God from the beginning; namely, to know ourselves in Spirit and in truth, even as we are known by God. ("Let us make man in our image and after our likeness.")

18

The Antichrist

"Then shall many false prophets arise and deceive many. And because inequity shall abound the loves of many shall wax cold."

MATTHEW 24:11,12

As we continue to learn more about the mind's three states of reality, we should not forget that all form, whether visible or invisible, exists as structured symbolism. All life is expressed through symbolism and resides in a symbolic state. It is the Life within the symbol that quickens. Of itself, the symbol profits nothing. ("Of myself I can do nothing. It is the Father within me that does the work.") In keeping with this outpouring of mirrored imagery, any change in its character results in a change in the mind's reality. ("When I was a child, I thought as a child; but when I became a man, I put away childish things.") Any renewing of the mind therefore requires a conversion of the mind's symbolism.

It is important to understand how symbolism relates to life, for without the interaction of these figurative entities there would be neither evolution nor involution. Since transforming invisible Spirit into visible substance is central to God's work, symbolism's true light is colorfully arrayed and expressed in every conceivable way. All the while, its principle maintains its inherent harmony.

Typically, we see the serpent characterized in Eden's Tree of Knowledge of good and evil reappearing, after some four thousand years, as the Antichrist, *as an entity of darkness that is opposed to light.* In the same manner, the light characterized by Eden's Tree of Life reappears as God's true light, his Christ. Thus, by way of symbolic substitution, we see that when Adam and Eve ate of the forbidden fruit, *the externalizing of the mind's knowledge and reality,* Antichrist assumed temporal authority over man. And when Jesus ascended to the Father, *by eating of the Tree of Life,* all power in heaven and earth was given to man. ("All power is given to me in heaven and on earth.") Once we understand the interconnecting principle of symbolism, the timeline is removed and all appearances become symbolic. All can therefore be transposed into the "now." ("Judge not by *reasonable* appearance, but judge right judgment.")

The perception that temporal darkness, which is identified with the Antichrist, did not enter the world until after the crucifixion of Jesus of Nazareth is obviously a misnomer. Christ's crucifixion within man began in Eden and continues to this day. Likewise, the deceptions of the Antichrist that began in Eden continue to this day. We should not be deceived. The veiled faces of symbolism should not cloud the mind. Conversely, the Son of man comes with clouds. ("Behold, he comes with clouds, *clouded symbolism,* bringing all the holy angels, *bringing his veiled symbolic truths,* with him.") The same is expressed in the book of Job, which relates, "And now men see not the bright light that is in the clouds, except the Spirit passes and cleanses them." It is thus given to, *"whosoever will,"* to be caught up with the Son of man in the clouds, *in his veiled symbolism.* So shall we ever be with the Lord.

Perhaps the symbol that best personifies the darkness of Antichrist is the word "deception;" he that deceives all nations. Recognizably, the power that sits in the seat of deception is the faculty of temporal Reason. It is here that the face of the elusive Antichrist is unveiled. The disciple John speaks of temporal Reason perverting the gospel of Christ when he writes:

"It is the last time; and as you have heard the Antichrist, *the deceiver,* shall come. Even now there are many Antichrists, *many deceivers,* within the world. ('Many false prophets shall arise and deceive many.')

They went out from us, but they were not of us, for if they had been of us, they would no doubt have continued with us. But they went out from us that their works might be made manifest."

Because division was prevalent even among the first Christians, Paul counseled, "Try the spirits; for any spirit that confesses not that Jesus Christ has come in the flesh, *teaches that God's image and likeness is not personified in man,* is not of God." Accordingly, he that denies the Christ, *the true light,* within himself affirms the Antichrist, *affirms the gross darkness that he personifies.*

Be assured that on a temporal level of understanding, for every negative action there is an equal negative reaction, a transferring of negative energy. Knowing this, Christ forewarned his disciples of the division his ministry would suffer at the hands of the Antichrist. Here are a few examples:

■ "Many shall come in my name, *falsifying my knowledge,* saying, I am the way. Go not after them, neither follow them.

For, as a great light that shines from east to west, so shall be
the coming of the Son of man."

■ "And because iniquity shall abound, the loves of many shall
wax cold. But he that endures to the end shall be saved."

■ "Not every one that says Lord, Lord, shall enter into the kingdom
of heaven; but he that does the will of my Father in heaven."

■ "In that day many shall say to me, Have we not prophesied in
your name? Have we not cast out devils and done many wonderful works in your name? And I shall say to them, Depart
from me, you workers of iniquity. I never knew you."

■ "I say unto you, watch! For if the good man of the house had
known at what hour the thief would come, he would not have
allowed his house to be broken into and his goods spoiled."

■ "They divided his garments amongst them, and for his vesture they did cast lots."

It is now some two thousand years since Christ, *God's Word,*
was personified in the person of Jesus of Nazareth, and all that
he foretold has been fulfilled. The pseudo-spiritual mind, the
stumbling stone, the captive exile, and the Antichrist all remain
with us. The cross that was to deliver mankind from affliction
weighs heavily upon the shoulders of us all. The mystery of
Christ's crucifixion still veils the path to life eternal and the great
tribulation continues.

But this is not the end; it only precedes a new beginning.
There is a Spiritual resurrection! There is the dawning of a new
day! And the wonder of it all is that God has not failed to show us
the way. ("I will never leave you nor forsake you.") He has opened
wide the gates to his eternal kingdom and invited every man,
woman and child coming into the world to enter. As John writes
in his Revelation, "The gates of the holy city shall not be closed by
day; and there shall be no night there. For the Lord God gives its
inhabitants light; and his Christ is the light thereof."

19

Revelation

> "How great are the signs of God and how mighty are his wonders! His kingdom is an everlasting kingdom and his dominion is from generation to generation."
>
> DANIEL 4:3

T he language of God and his Universe is symbolism. There is no place his voice is not heard. All bears his image and likeness. In keeping with this unity, when God created man as the centerpiece of his work all symbolism witnessed to him. ("Let all the angels of God, *all the similes of God,* witness to him.") Therein, man became a parallelism, *a simile,* an entity whose Spiritual substance was equal to the indwelling light that appeared within Creation. God, Man and Creation's true light thus shared a common image and likeness. All was Spirit made flesh. ("Come, beloved of my Father, and inherit the kingdom that was prepared for you from the foundation of the world.")

Judeo-Christian thought correlates this unity through the revelatory patterns that appear within God's Word, *the Wordbody of Christ.* The Book of Revelation therefore begins with the introduction, "The revelation of Jesus Christ, *the Word similes of*

Christ, which God gave to Christ to show unto his servants, *those who conform to his knowledge,* those things which must shortly come to pass." That is, God had enlisted John to show unto his servants how things not previously seen, *in the Word's first reading,* should henceforth appear, *in the Word's second reading.* As Jesus told his disciples, "There is nothing hidden that shall not be brought to light." Accordingly, upon entering the Word's revelatory body, the *temporal* things that were, the *pseudo-spiritual* things that are, and the *Spiritual* things yet to come, are all recognized as correlated symbolism. ("Jesus spoke in parables, *in comparisons,* and without a parable spoke he not unto them.") The transposed light of Life within symbolic form is thus recognized as Christ's eternal dwelling place. ("I am the Life.")

Once we recognize that all of God's work is based upon correlated symbolism, things that relate to the time-space continuum are of no consequence. It is the Life within the symbolism that quickens, the faces of symbolism are only Life's façade. ("And when the voice of the seventh angel shall begin to sound, *whose voice is heard in the Word's second reading,* time shall be no longer, as he has declared to his servants the prophets.")

We thus discover that just as Creation witnessed to the inherent light of Life within its midst through the use of symbolic comparisons, so Christ witnessed to the light of Life within mankind's midst through the use of symbolic comparisons. ("Whatsoever the Father does, the Son does likewise.") Thus, through the transposing of symbolic imagery, *through revelations acquired from pseudo-spiritual similes,* mankind's everlasting glory was revealed by the Son of man, and the reality that accompanied that glory became man's exceeding great reward. ("I am your exceeding great reward.")

Since Scripture has both a linear and a parallel reading, it is not surprising that in man's linear world John's Book of Revelation, which in its entirety is a parallelism, is by far the most misunderstood book of the Bible. For the uninitiated it is the most complex of Scripture's presentations. Actually, John's revelation is presented as an epilogue. He employs symbolism to correlate the symbolism previously used by Moses, the prophets, and the Son of man. Notably, two witnesses were needed to verify the completion of that earlier work. The writings of the apostles of Christ provided a first witness and John's Book of Revelation provided a second witness. Therefore, as the last of the Bible's prophetical books, John's prophecies confirm the fulfilling of the law and the prophets and the conclusion of Christ's revelatory ministry. Since John uses Spiritual symbolism to explain Spiritual symbolism, until such time as the mind becomes adept at interpreting parallel imagery, the book of Revelation should be approached cautiously. Misguided interpretations of his work only compound the mind's division and become counterproductive.

Before attempting to understand John's complex imagery the reader should steel himself against its brash appearance. The book's frightening visions must not be allowed to destroy its truth. We must be constantly aware that John is using aphorisms to confuse and provoke the mind's corrupt imagination. ("I shall confound the wise and bring to nothing the understanding of the prudent.") Paul refers to this masking of truth when he writes, "He has chosen weak things, and foolish things, and things that are not to bring to nothing the things that are." Beneath the book's veiled facade, the disciple follows the pattern set forth in the law and the prophets. Therefore, when all of the masks are removed from his similes, we find John's revelation expounding the mind's continuing three states of reality. As in all prophecy, the faces revealed are none other than our own. The imagery within his work is thus recognized as a veiling of parallelisms.

John introduces his revelation by addressing the problems of the seven churches that are in Asia Minor, therein signaling the

Word's continuing division within the pseudo-spiritual mind. As overseer of the seven churches, John envisions Christ as he that holds the seven stars in his right hand and walks among the seven golden candlesticks, *as he that witness to Life's all-inclusive unity and conveys that unity to pseudo-spiritual man.* He then discloses that the seven stars in Christ's right hand are the angels of the seven churches, *the instructional truths sent by God that witness to his unity,* and the seven golden candlesticks wherein he walks are the seven churches, *the pseudo-spiritual levels of thought to which those truths witness.* Directing his vision toward the false interpretations the seven churches have adopted, Christ chastens the angels for allowing God's truth to be falsified. ("Do you not know you are to judge angels?")

The misconduct of the seven angels and the seven pseudo-spiritual churches is selectively expressed in the following:

- "To the angel of the church at Ephesus: I am somewhat against you because you have left your first love, *you have strayed from the truth.* Remember from where you have fallen and repent or I will come and remove your candlestick from out of its place."
- "To the angel of the church at Pergamos: I have a few things against you; for you have those among you that teach the doctrine of Balaam, *I shall behold him, but not now, I shall see him, but not nigh.* They lay a stumbling block before my chosen people. Repent; or I will come quickly and will fight against you with the sword of my mouth, *the Word of truth.*"
- "To the angel of the church at Sardis: I have not found your works perfect before God. I know that you have a name that you live, *a knowledge that is false that you live,* and you are dead. Therefore, if you do not watch and repent, I will come to you as a thief; and you shall not know at what hour I will come."

■ "To the angel of the church at Laodiceans: I know your works, that you are neither hot nor cold. So, because you are only lukewarm, I will spew you out of my mouth. You say you are rich and increased with goods and have need of nothing, but you are miserable, and poor, and blind, and naked. As many as I love I rebuke and chasten; be zealous therefore and repent."

As John enlarges upon the conflict existing between the mind's Spiritual and pseudo-spiritual realities, he introduces countless masked faces. He envisions God's glory as a throne set in heaven, before which appears a sea of glass, *a see of transparent truth,* clear as crystal. Before the throne and the sea of glass sit the twenty-four *pseudo-spiritual* church elders, *the church's firstborn,* and in the midst of the throne and round about the throne, *in the midst of God's glory and round about his glory,* he sees four *temporal-minded* beasts. And when the beasts, *the temporal aspect of God's signs and wonders,* convert and give glory and thanks to him that sits upon the throne, *the Creator,* the pseudo-spiritual elders cast their crowns, *their latent truths,* before him. John thus uses metaphors to characterize the passage of God's Word from an external to internal reading.

As his revelation unfolds, he sees a book that is written in heaven, *the Word's second reading,* a book that no man is prepared to open and to look upon, *a symbolism that the temporal mind is unable to comprehend.* A Lamb, *the Christ,* then appears in the midst of the throne, in the midst of God's glory and in the midst of the beasts and the elders, *in the midst of the mind's first two realities,* having the seven Spirits of God sent forth into all the earth. When the Lamb takes the book, *Scripture's second reading,* from him who sits upon the throne, all that are present fall down before him and sing a new song saying that only the Lamb, *the mind of Christ,* is worthy to break the seals and to open the book. By using the metaphor that only the Lamb is worthy to understand God's higher truth, John reinforces Christ's disclosure that God has committed all judgment to his Word. ("The Father judges no man, but has committed all judgment to the Son.")

When the Lamb opens God's sealed Word, *the Word's second reading*, the affect is Apocalyptic. All of the Bible's mysteries, from Genesis through the writings of the apostles, become undone. All is unveiled for mankind to look upon. As the seals are progressively removed, the mysteries involving mankind *incrementally* come to light:

- When the first seal is opened, a crown is given to man, *his image and likeness in God,* and he goes forth conquering and to conquer.
- When the second seal is opened, having descended into temporal darkness man receives power to take peace from the earth and to kill his fellow man, and a great sword, *of pseudo-spiritual truth,* is given him.
- When the third seal is opened, "reasonable judgment" is released upon the earth, *re: the law of Moses,* and all is bought and sold by weight and measure.
- When the fourth seal is opened, Death and Hell ravage the earth, *the desolations incurred at the judging of Israel and the nations.* They kill with the sword, *of false judgment,* with hunger and with death.
- When the fifth seal is opened, the Son of man is recognized as dwelling in the midst of pseudo-spiritual truth, and the souls of those who suffered death for the Word of God and for the testimony that they held, *the dead in Christ,* are recognized. But they are told that they must rest for a season, until such time as their brethren, who would be killed as they were, should be fulfilled. *This event signals the quickening of*

the prophets and the approaching "end time," when all would coalesce into a united Christ Consciousness.

- When the sixth seal is opened, true Spiritual judgment descends from heaven in the person of Christ, and the Word is made flesh. The stars, *the angels of mankind's lesser light,* fall from heaven and the earth is shaken. The mountains are moved from their places and the mighty men of the earth, *the mind's false prophets,* seek shelter amongst the rocks saying, "Hide us from the wrath of the Lamb, *from the light of eternal truth,* and from the face of him that sits upon the throne."

- When the seventh seal is opened, there is silence in heaven for a short period, and the angels of God prepare to trumpet their glory. The seventh angel then fills his golden censer with fire, *with the Spirit of truth,* from the altar and casts it into the earth. Voices and thundering and lightning and a great quaking of the earth then follow. The seven angels of God, *the myriad truths within his work,* then go forth to remove all things that offend.

John's apocalyptic vision of Scripture thus translates into a synoptic view of the mind's three states of reality. The sealing of God's Word in the foreheads of the twelve tribes of Israel, twelve thousand of each tribe or one hundred and forty-four thousand in all, refers to the sowing of God's redemptive work into Israel through the law and the prophets. *The number "twelve" is used as a symbol for judgment.* Thereafter, all nations, kindred and people, a multitude that no man can number, are brought into the Word's Spiritual fold. ("Other sheep have I, not of this fold. Them I must bring also and there shall be one fold and one shepherd.") These have cleansed their thoughts in the wellspring of God's eternal truth and have come out of the great tribulation that afflicts all nations.

At length, the seventh angel appears before John and places a rod in his hand with which he is to measure the truths of God, and the angel says:

"Rise, and measure the temple of God, *the Word-body of Christ,* and the *pseudo-spiritual* altar; and those who bear witness therein, *the angels beneath the alter that witness to his truth.* But the court that is without the temple, *the mind that courts life externally,* leave out; for it is given to the Gentiles, *the temporal mind,* and the holy city, *the Word of truth,* they shall tread under foot, *they shall judge without Spiritual understanding."*

Thereafter, John envisions the death and resurrection of God's two witnesses. *They are the signs and wonders witnessed by the law and the prophets that were counted as slain but raised in Spirit and in truth with the quickening of the Son of man.* With their resurrection, *with the fulfilling of their testimony,* the temple of God in heaven is opened and the Ark of the Testimony, *the truth of their testimony,* appears in his temple.

John then turns his thoughts toward "Babylon the great." He likens her lies to a blasphemous and adulterous woman, *the temporal mind,* who sits upon a beast having seven heads and ten horns, *signifying pseudo-spiritual thought.* She feigns righteousness by witnessing to works created by her own hands, and she drinks from a golden cup full of filth and abominations, *full of lies and deceptions.* The disciple relates, "In her was found the blood of the prophets, of the saints, and of all that were slain upon the earth." She comes to her end when her body is given to the burning flame, *the Word's fiery truth,* and the beast *of lies* upon which she rides is destroyed. With her demise, man then obtains salvation.

After employing a wide variety of symbolic imagery John concludes his assault against the mind's temporal and pseudo-spiritual realities with the metaphor, "And fire, *the Spirit of truth,* came down from God out of heaven and destroyed them all." The fiery end that consumes the mind's evil nature reflects Christ's warning, "I have come not to bring peace upon the earth, but a sword. I baptize with fire and with the Holy Ghost."

John's report ultimately reaches the end to which all avenues of his revelation lead. Following the destruction of all things that offend, he writes:

"And I saw a new *Spiritual* heaven and a new *Spiritual* earth; for the first heaven and the first earth were passed away.

And I saw the holy city, the New Jerusalem, *the Spirit of truth,* coming down from God out of heaven, prepared as a bride, *a new mind,* adorned for her husband.

And I heard a great voice out of heaven saying, BEHOLD, THE TABERNACLE OF GOD IS WITH MEN, *God's all-inclusive unity is with men;* and he shall dwell with them, and they shall be his people."

Then, likening Christ's light within mankind's midst to the Tree of Life that appeared in the midst of Eden's Garden, John envisions this symbolic finale:

"And he showed me a pure river of water of Life, *a pure river of Spiritual truth,* clear as crystal, proceeding out of the throne of God and of the Lamb, *proceeding out of their Spiritual revelations.*

In the midst of the street of it and on either side of the river, *the river of everlasting truth,* was the Tree of Life, bearing twelve manner of fruits; *bearing true Spiritual judgment.* And the leaves of the tree, *the similes that covered its branches,* were for the healing of the nations, *were for the healing of the mind's division."*

For those who teach that John's revelation is a foretelling of worldly events I refer you to his closing summation:

"SEAL NOT THE SAYINGS OF THE PROPHESY OF THIS BOOK, FOR THE TIME IS AT HAND.

He that is unjust, let him be unjust still; and he that is filthy, let him be filthy still; and he that is righteous, let him be righteous still; and he that is holy, let him be holy still.

Behold, I come quickly; and my reward is with me, to give to every man according to his works."

John's Book of Revelation obviously answers one of the most important questions put forth by Christ's disciples: "Lord, tell us when these things shall be and what shall be the sign of your coming?" Regrettably, the world has failed to see the bright light that radiates from Christ's clouded similes. ("A cloud received him up out of their sight.") Until now, Jew and Christian alike continue to await his coming, or his return. Both fail to hear his voice. Both remain dedicated to pseudo-spiritual traditions that deny his truth. Thus, eternal death and eternal life continue to dwell side by side. It is no wonder that Christ became disheartened with his people when they said, "Lord, show us a sign, *a simile,* and we shall believe." And so the long night of unbelief continues.

20

The Pattern

"That things on earth might serve as a shadow of heavenly things, the Lord instructed Moses to follow the pattern that was shown to him on the mount."

HEBREWS 8:5

We often overlook the obvious. What we cannot physically see, we are inclined to view as otherworldly. Yet we have only to look inward to realize that we ourselves are otherworldly. Our knowledge, our reality and our genetic consistency are all invisible to the naked eye. Indeed, this otherworldly realm of invisible intelligence in which we reside is responsible for creating the countless visible and invisible forms that constitute modern civilization. It is absurd to perceive ourselves primarily as visible beings. Are we totally mindless? Have we forgotten that what appears is only an image and likeness of the mind's invisible world? Must we be reminded that the invisible is the quickening power? Two thousand years ago, Jesus reminded the Jews of this disparity when he said, "It is the Spirit that quickens. The flesh profits nothing."

The book of Hebrews theologically expounds that through faith we understand that things seen were not made by things that do appear. How the author of Hebrews concludes that faith is essential to understanding the obvious is baffling. Does it take faith to understand that form is incapable of self-creation? What became of common sense? Faith is a vehicle of transport, not an end in itself. We trust that faith will take us from what we have not to what we hope to have. Consider man's workmanship. Should faith be factored into what we experience mentally as normal productivity? The point is moot. When we allow faith to circumvent common sense, we place its strength in jeopardy. Faith should serve as needed, not be placed in our path as a stumbling block. As Scripture relates, "Show me your works and I will know your faith by your works."

The books of the Bible unanimously support the principle that consciousness determines form. That is, the inherent Life within consciousness is responsible for the visible forms it creates. Accordingly, when Moses was instructed to build the tabernacle of God after the pattern shown to him on the mount, the structure that he raised became a replica of what he Spiritually envisioned within himself. God's pseudo-spiritual tabernacle was thus raised in the image and likeness of the human frame.

In keeping with this pattern, when Moses ascended into Sinai and communed with God concerning the pattern of his dwelling place, he never left the mount. Are we to understand, then, that God conjured up some mystical vision within the mind of Moses? Not at all. What Moses recognized from his Spiritual exchanges on Sinai was the corresponding imagery that related man to his Creator. ("Take the shoes from off your feet, *uncover your understanding,* for the ground on which you stand is holy ground.") Transposing that pattern into symbolic manifestation, he then fashioned the tabernacle in the wilderness and overlaid it with skins, *a simile of the tabernacle that resided in the wilderness of mankind's pseudo-spiritual consciousness.*

With the conversion of his knowledge into three distinct levels of thought, a progressive trilogy was imparted to mankind, a trilogy that held the keys to achieving unity with God. ("To him that overcomes I will give the keys to the kingdom of heaven; and he shall go no more out.") The truth that God intended mankind to share in Life's recurring pattern is seen in the following:

- Life's pattern within man appears as an image and likeness, *a simile of what it represents.* Personifying that pattern, Jesus said, "I am in the Father and the Father is in me. He that has seen me has seen the Father."
- A pattern is a parallelism, *a comparison, a comparable.* "The Son of man therefore spoke in parables, *in Spiritual patterns,* and without a parable spoke he not unto them."
- A pattern is a vehicle of conveyance, *a vehicle of passover, or crossover.* Christ therefore explained, "No man comes to the Father except by me."
- A pattern is an outlined facsimile. Expressing that accord, Christ said, "All that the Father has are mine."
- A pattern is a transposing of things not seen. "No man has seen the Father. The only begotten, *the pattern,* which is in the bosom of the Father, he has declared him."

These comparisons further corroborate that what Moses saw within himself at Sinai was the inherent pattern that accompanied God's work, an attribute of the true light that was embodied within mankind. This characteristic was acknowledged by the Son of man when he told the Jews, "If you had believed Moses you would have known me; for Moses spoke of me."

The authority delegated to this revelatory pattern is seen when substitution is used to correlate the opening lines of John's Gospel. His introduction then reads:

"In the beginning was the Word, *the pattern,* and the Word, *the pattern,* was with God, and the Word, *the pattern,* was God.

All things were made by him, *patterned after his inherent principles,* and without him, *without the principles within his pattern,* was not anything made that was made.

In him, *in his pattern,* was Life, and the Life was the light of men."

Paul also correlates the pattern shared among God, Christ and man when he speaks of man obtaining "the mind of Christ." He recognized that in sharing that pattern, man received power to become "the brightness of the Father's glory and the express image of his person." Accordingly, the apostle counseled his followers to share in the glory of God's pattern, just as Moses had counseled Israel to share in the glory that God had imparted to him in recognizing that pattern.

This sharing of Spiritual knowledge opens the door to another misunderstood facet of Scripture's Word; namely, the Son of man's promised return in his Father's kingdom. This is again clarified through Spiritual translation. The promised imminent arrival of Christ in his Father's glory is expressed in the following:

■ "Seek first the kingdom of God, *the pattern of God,* and his righteousness and all these things shall be added to you."
■ "The kingdom of God, *the pattern of God,* comes not with observation; neither shall they say, Look here! Or, Look there! For the kingdom of God, *the pattern of God,* is within you."
■ "A kingdom, *a pattern,* divided against itself cannot stand."

- "You shall see Abraham, Isaac and Jacob, and all the prophets, set down in the kingdom, *the pattern*, of heaven; but you yourselves shall be thrust out."
- "The kingdoms, *the Spiritual patterns*, of this world have become the kingdoms, *the Spiritual patterns*, of our God and of his Christ."
- "I shall not drink of the fruit of the vine until I drink it new with you in my Father's kingdom, *in my Father's pattern*."

The pattern that Moses was instructed to follow also applies to aphorisms used to signify God's cloud. Here are a few examples:

- "Behold, I set my bow, *my glory*, in the cloud, *in the pattern*, and I shall look upon it in the day of rain."
- "They shall see the Son of man coming in the clouds, *the patterns*, of heaven with power and great glory."
- "With so great a cloud, *a pattern*, of witnesses, let us run the race that is set before us."
- "And now men see not the bright light that is in the cloud, *in the pattern*, except the wind, *the Spirit*, passes and cleanses them."
- "A cloud, *a pattern*, received him up out of their sight."

One of the great wonders of Scripture is its correlative unity. It resounds with the music of the spheres. It is only when the Word is reduced to religious tradition and discordant doctrine that its unity is sacrificed.

The importance of these Spiritual patterns is further emphasized when John discloses, "No man has ever seen the Father. The only begotten, *the pattern of truth*, which is in the bosom of the Father, he has declared him." John specifically makes the point that God, as an all-encompassing macrocosm, was visually unapproachable. He writes, "No man has ever seen the Father." He then informs us that in an effort to characterize his Spirit, the Creator has translated his image and likeness into signs and wonders, *into Word-similes or Word-patterns,* to which man can relate. ("The only begotten which is in the bosom of the Father, he has declared him.") Reflective of Scripture's consistent progression, we thus see John linking the pattern of man's Spiritual quickening to Isaiah's simile of the birth of the Son of man. ("Unto us a child is born, unto us a Son is given; and he shall be called the mighty God, the everlasting Father, the Prince of Peace.")

Correlating his knowledge with events surrounding that Age, John realized the pattern of signs and wonders that witnessed to the Son of man in the law and the prophets, had evolved and was now personified in the Word-body of Jesus Christ. ("And the Word made flesh and dwelt among us; and we beheld his glory as the only begotten of the Father, full of grace and truth.") In that context, John recognized that Scripture's Word-pattern was made flesh long before the advent of Christ in the person of Jesus of Nazareth. This tenet becomes apparent in the following:

- From Adam until Moses, the Word-pattern was made flesh in God's outpictured signs and wonders.
- From Moses until Israel's entry into the Promised Land, the Word-pattern was made flesh in the laws and statutes housed in the tabernacle in the wilderness.
- From Israel's entry into the Promised Land until the advent of the prophets, the Word-pattern was made flesh in the earthy fulfillment of God's promises to Abraham.
- From the prophets until John the Baptist, the Word-pattern was made flesh in the desolations of Jerusalem and the predictions of the prophets.
- From the birth of Jesus Christ until his reappearing in the Holy Ghost, the Word-pattern was made flesh in the signs and wonders of the Son of man's ministry.

In all, John perceived God's progressive work as a symbolic conjunction, an ongoing parallelism, *or pattern,* whose predestined role was to quicken visible form and translate it into invisible Spirit.

To bring God's outpictured work into sharper focus Jesus asked his disciples, "Who do men say that I, the Son of man, am?" And Peter answered, "You are the Christ, the Son, *the Word-pattern,* of the living God." Upon hearing Peter's insightful response, Jesus responded, "Man has not revealed this to you, Peter, but my Father which is in heaven. This is the rock, *the confirmation of God's Word-pattern in man,* and sure foundation that I will build upon, and the gates of hell shall not prevail against it." As explained throughout these pages, the principle of God's Spirit abiding in man is unalterable. All else lies.

Notwithstanding, the world remains in the throes of religious division. Man fails to comprehend the importance of the prophet's insight, "They shall all be taught of God." ("When the Spirit of truth has come, he shall lead you into all truth.") We can only hope that with growing Spiritual enlightenment, mankind's doctrinal misconceptions will soon end. Time may obscure the Spiritual pattern that God has provided for man's instruction, but its truth shall remain forever. There is a time and a season for everything born under the sun, but the Creator's directives are eternal and shall not pass away. ("Heaven and earth shall pass away, but my words shall not pass away.")

21

Fulfillment

"And Jesus came into Galilee preaching the gospel of the kingdom of God, saying, The time is fulfilled. The kingdom of God is at hand. Believe the Scriptures."

MARK 1:15

It is a paradox that the Judeo-Christian community has so many believers and still continues to journey under a cloud of unbelief. Generation after generation passes through this world and all fail to understand that you cannot serve doctrine and serve God. Certainly, man was not made to serve doctrine, *the Sabbath,* but doctrine was made to serve man. ("The law was our schoolmaster to bring us to Christ.") Doctrine, like faith, should transport the believer from what they Spiritually lack to what God desires them to have; in this case, residency in his kingdom. To that end, all pseudo-spiritual doctrines fail miserably. Why? Because they are founded upon reasonable judgment, on what appears reasonable to the pseudo-spiritual mind. Jesus refers to this failure in the following parable:

"Every one that hears my sayings and fails to reconcile them to himself, shall be as a foolish man which built his house upon the sand:

And the rains descended, and the floods came, and the winds blew and beat upon the house, and it fell; and great was the fall of it."

Until doctrine is Spiritually translated and purged of its dross, it remains lifeless; and because the doctrine is lifeless, the believer is also left without Life. ("The servant is not greater than the master.")

But this does not imply that Judeo-Christian doctrine is flawed and should be abolished. The Word of eternal Life was instituted by God and provided mankind with Spiritual principles upon which he has since built. ("Since by man came death, by man came also the resurrection of the dead.") The problem encountered along the way was that both Jew and Christian transformed God's Word from a vehicle of revelation into articles of worship. Swayed by the temporal mind, "The people changed their glory into the likeness of an ox." Submitting to estranged entities, they have perceived God's instruction as a progression of moral decrees and far-off promises. As history records, that tragic mistake was followed by a wilderness journey that continues to this day.

In a biblical sense, the words "law" and "doctrine" are interchangeable. The common ground shared by these two descriptions becomes apparent in the following quotations:

■ "The law, *the external doctrine of God*, was our schoolmaster to bring us to Christ, *the internal doctrine of God*."

■ "Think not that I have come to destroy the law and the prophets, *the external doctrine of God,* but to fulfill them, *through the internal doctrine of God's Spirit."*

■ "The law and the prophets, *the external doctrine of God,* was until John. Now the kingdom of God, *the internal doctrine of God,* is preached."

■ "Moses gave you the law, *the external doctrine of God,* but none of you keep it. Why do you go about to kill me? *the internal doctrine of God."*

■ "For Christ is the end of the law, *the internal fulfillment of the external doctrine of God."*

■ "It is not the hearers of the law's traditional aspect, *the external doctrine of God,* that are guiltless before the Lord, but the doers of the law's Spiritual aspect, *the doers of the internal doctrine of God,* that are justified."

■ "Your law, *your internal doctrine,* O Lord, is in my heart."

Many Christians are falsely taught that because Christ has fulfilled the law of God they no longer need its counsel. What they fail to understand is that you cannot separate Christ from the law. Christ is not only the Word of the law, but the true light that is in the law. ("The law of Life.") Has humanity advanced so far that it no longer requires a Spiritual schoolmaster? Has God's instructional Word become obsolete? Can man, who is identified by his knowledge, attain eternal consciousness without having Spiritual instruction? I think not! The mind of Christ is rooted in the signs and wonders that comprise the law and the prophets. The internal light that follows their external testimony is no doubt Spiritually preferable, but having obtained the fruits of their labors, we should not destroy the tree they so diligently planted and nurtured. ("Other men have labored and you are entered into their labors.") We need only to remove the tree's "suckers."

Evidence that God had no intention of dismissing the law and the prophets, *the Word's external witness,* and that his signs and wonders would be raised to a higher level of understanding, *the Word's internal witness,* is recognized in the following:

- "Those who have been with me in the *internal* regeneration shall sit upon twelve thrones and judge the twelve *external* tribes of Israel."
- "There are *external* first that shall be last; and there are *internal* last that shall be first."
- "I saw thrones, and they sat upon them, and *internal* judgment was given to them."
- "I will lay *internal* judgment to the line and righteousness to the plummet, and the hail shall sweep away the *external* refuge of lies."
- "He that seeks his life *internally* must lose it *externally.* And he that loses his life *externally* shall find it *internally* unto life eternal."
- "I have power to lay down my *external* life and I have power to take it up again *internally.*"
- "If I go to prepare a place for you *internally* I will come again to receive you unto myself; that where I am *internally* there you may be also."

In keeping with these random examples, Scripture confirms, "He that receives the Son has the witness of God in himself." ("His Spirit bears witness with our Spirit that we are the Sons of God.")

We thus see the culmination of Christ's ministry creating a supernatural parallelism. For just as God initially translated the *internal* pattern of his Spirit into *external* signs and wonders, we now see Christ, in an inverse manner, translating the *external* pattern of his Spirit into *internal* signs and wonders. United as two in one body, they then reappear as the Holy Ghost. ("What

God has joined together let not man put asunder.") Thus by reversing the flow of the Creator's work, Christ brings the king-dom of God to fruition in man. ("You shall go in and out and find pasture.") Paul therefore explains, "All is raised in its own order." First Christ, the first fruit, *the external witness of the Son of man;* then those who are Christ's at his *internal* coming, *his appearing with the Father in the Holy Ghost.* Therein, Christ and Man inherit the external and internal content of God's Spirit. ("He that overcomes shall inherit all things.")

Having recognized that God's externalized signs and wonders are internalized in Christ, we are confronted with what initially appears as a contradiction: the truth that Creation's external appearance, which from Adam forward was counted as darkness and death, in the end is revealed as the tabernacle of God's true light. This inconsistency is resolved once we understand that Scripture unfolds as a reconciling work. In the beginning God's light was made to shine in formal darkness and the darkness comprehended it not. In the end, through reconciliation, this same light is made to shine out of darkness, clothed anew as the brightness of God's internal glory and the express image of his person. ("Heaven and earth are full of his glory.")

What essentially changes in this new scenario is man's per-ception of Creation's content. When the veil of outer appear-ance is removed and Creation's substance is viewed in a Spiritual context, all is quickened and passed from darkness into light. ("There shall be no night there; for the Lord God gives them light.") When we transpose the creative process into our-selves, God's unity with all things is confirmed. Just as the senses translate their perceptions into temporal knowledge, so the signs and wonders of God translate their messages into pseudo-spiritual knowledge. In turn, pseudo-spiritual knowledge trans-lates its message into Spiritual knowledge and man attains "the mind of Christ." Thereafter, the light of Spiritual knowledge recognizes its face in all that God has made, and the light of Life appears as all in all.

The truth that man was destined to personify the two witnessing aspects in all of the Creator's work is expressed in the following:

- "And Elisha picked up Elijah's mantle, *the outer covering of Elijah's spirit,* and with it he smote the Jordan, *the pseudospiritual waters of the lower Jordan,* saying, Where is the Lord God of Elijah? And the waters of the lower Jordan were parted so that Elisha passed over on dry land."
- "A light, *the light of Spiritual truth in man,* is not brought forth to be placed under a bushel, *hidden in darkness,* but to be set on a lamp stand so that all who are in the house may see."
- "I have come into the world as a light, that you should not abide in darkness."
- "Walk in the light and, therein, become children, *expressions,* of the light"
- "In the Son of man was Life; and the Life was the light of men. And the light shines in darkness."
- "The light of the body is the eye, *the 'I' of knowledge.* If your eye, *your knowledge,* is single, *one with God's Spirit,* your whole body shall be full of light."
- "I am the light of the world. He that seeks me shall have the light of Life."
- "You are the light of the world. A city that is set upon a hill cannot be hid."

Two thousand years have elapsed since Jesus assured the Jews, "This generation shall not pass until all that I have spoken is fulfilled." Notwithstanding, the eyes of humanity continue to search the heavens for the coming of their Redeemer. They cannot accept Christ's declaration, "The time is fulfilled; the kingdom of God is at hand." In keeping with the various aspects of linear progression, new generations are born and pass away, but the truths uttered by Christ remain. As promised, all is fulfilled; even the error he asserted could not be fulfilled bows to his truth. Yet, man persists in dreaming his own impossible dream. ("They shall surely gather together, but not by me.")

22

Discovering the Eternal

"The Lord of hosts has prepared a great feast for all the people in his glorious mountain of truth.

In his holy mountain the veil of covering that was spread over all nations shall be destroyed.

Death shall be swallowed up with victory; and the Lord God will wipe away the tears from all faces."

ISAIAH 25:6-8

It is puzzling that the Creator should be so close to us and yet seem so far away. In many ways, God seems aloof, yet he is readily available if we understand how to approach him. My own experience is that he communicates through Spiritual principles. When our thoughts coincide with his principles, he reacts. When they do not, there is silence. Jesus gave mankind a broad overview of what those principles involved when he said, "I am the Way, the Truth, and the Life. Ask anything in my name, *anything consistent with my knowledge,* and I will give it to you." Since Christ's life is a revelation of the Father's Life, we must assume that what he said also applies to communicating and receiving gifts from God. Indeed, the whole purpose of Christ's ministry was to instill the harmonious tenets of the Creator's principles in mankind.

Humanity is faced with a dilemma because the Word of God, *the vehicle wherein Life's eternal principles are revealed,* must be Spiritually interpreted. So the question arises, "How can the pseudo-spiritual mind, much less the temporal mind, communicate with God through principles it fails to understand?" Jesus makes no mention of this impasse when he invites mankind to "freely take of the waters of Life." Consequently, his invitation to attend the Word's Spiritual "Feast of Lights" goes without response. The following parable draws our attention to this disparaging situation. Note that without translation, the King, his Son, the King's servants and those who comprise his kingdom are without identity. All is a simile. All must be translated before entry into the kingdom of heaven can be achieved.

"The kingdom of heaven is like unto a certain King, *God,* which made a marriage feast for his Son, *Christ;* and he sent his servants, *the Spiritual truths witnessed in the Law of Moses,* to call them he wished to attend the wedding. But they would not come.

So he sent his servants a second time, *the Spiritual truths witnessed by the prophets,* and the servants again told them that the King had prepared a great feast and that they should attend. But they made light of it and all went their own way.

When the King heard of this he was angry. So, he said to his servants, The wedding is ready but those that were first invited were not worthy. Go, therefore, into the highways and invite those that you find; both good and bad. And the King's servants went forth as they were instructed and invited all that were in the way.

The wedding, and its festivities, was thus furnished with
guests other than those whom the King had first called."

We thus see that God is not beyond turning away the world's
many spiritual pretenders while revealing himself to those who
were yet without knowledge of his Spiritual ways. Therein,
"Many are called but few are chosen."

I was once asked what I thought was the most difficult part
of growing Spiritually. I hesitated for only a moment before
replying, "Unlearning!" I have spent a lifetime unlearning secular error. I am ashamed to say that many times I stubbornly
refused to give up my old beliefs, until the weight of evidence
against them was so overwhelming I could no longer endure
their weight. Jesus emphasized the necessity for discarding the
temporal errors that afflict the pseudo-spiritual mind when he
said, "Except a corn of wheat fall into the ground and die, it
abides alone; but, if it die, it brings forth much fruit." Of all the
Spiritual tenets I have learned along the way, there is none more
important than this: Life and knowledge are inseparable. You
cannot inherit eternal Life without inheriting eternal knowledge.
Therefore, he that seeks perfection must forfeit the imperfections of the temporal and pseudo-spiritual mind. The illusory
thoughts that divide heaven and earth must be eliminated; there
is no other way. ("Be, therefore, perfect, even as your Father in
heaven is perfect.")

But how is this renewal of the mind to be attained? It is not
easy. It takes honesty, sincerity and true dedication. You must
have an open mind and respond only to the still small voice of
God's counsel. ("They shall all be taught of God.") Consider for a
moment that Jesus said, "My sheep know my voice and they will
not follow another." Then consider that there are several hundred
conflicting Judeo-Christian divisions of thought within the

world. Something is terribly wrong! Paul asked, "If the trumpet makes an uncertain sound, who will run to the battle?" So the question looms, "How, then, can we distinguish between what is right and what is wrong?" Scripture provides the answer when it says, "The Lord's Spirit bears witness with our Spirit." That is, they two become one flesh, a marriage made in heaven. Agreeably then, he that looks upon the face of God beholds his own true face as in a glass. ("The Lord is my mirror.")

Personally, I have found that any serious effort to acquire true Spiritual unity with the Creator is quickly rewarded with additional Spiritual understanding. ("And of his goodness have we all received; and grace for grace.") This, of course, excludes justification of errors that attend pseudo-spiritual knowledge. Christ accounted for that exclusion when he said, "That born of the flesh is flesh, and that born of the Spirit is Spirit." Will-worship and religious doctrine belong to the flesh. Understanding the Word of truth belongs to the Spirit. The difference between secular worship and Spiritual understanding is reflected in the following:

"Christ said, The hour approaches when you shall neither worship the Father, *seek understanding of the Father,* in this mountain nor at Jerusalem. You worship, *you understand,* you know not what.

Salvation is of the Jews; and we should worship, *should understand,* what we know.

Believe me, the hour is at hand when true worshippers, *those who truly understand,* shall worship, *shall understand,* the Father in Spirit and in truth; for the Father seeks such to worship, *to understand,* him.

And he scolded the Jews saying, You hypocrites, well did Isaiah prophesy of you when he said, This people draws near

to me with their mouth and honors me with their lips; but
their heart is far from me. In vain do they worship me, teaching for doctrines the commandments of men."

Assuring mankind that to gain understanding was to gain
wisdom, the book of Proverbs reads, "Wisdom is the principal
thing. Therefore, get wisdom; and with all your getting, get
understanding."

Be aware, however, that just as we evolve incrementally in
temporal and pseudo-spiritual thought, so must we evolve incrementally in Spiritual thought. God speaks to us individually and
according to our level of comprehension. Time and again, we
discover Spiritual truths of which we had no prior knowledge,
and we wonder why they were not recognized at an earlier time.
It is a common experience. The answer to this phenomenon, of
course, is that we are participating in an eternal journey; and like
God, we are in the process of discovering our true Spiritual identity. When Jesus said, "And this is life eternal, to know God," he
might well have said, "And this is life eternal, to know your true
Self in God." For in that eternal state the "I" of the Father and the
"I" of the Sons of God are One. ("I AM that I AM.")

One of the many undetected facets of Spiritual study is that
Scripture provides not only for the mind's entrance into the
kingdom of heaven, but also provides a knowledge that translates into the tongue of angels. Unlike the myriad number of lan-
guages verbalized here on earth, there is but one tongue spoken
in heaven, the tongue of God: the tongue of symbolism. Jesus
spoke of man having conversations with those in heaven when
he said, "The children of the resurrection are equal to the angels
of heaven." That is, they relate to the truths, *the angels,* which
convey heaven's symbolism. Since heaven is a strange land to
those who dwell on earth, we should not expect to enter that

land without first learning the tongue of its inhabitants, and the Bible prepares us for that journey.

It thus follows that while the temporal mind prepares us to judge all things pertaining to the below, the Spiritual mind prepares us, *through the process of translation,* to judge all things in the above. In concert with the pattern set forth by Christ, those who enter God's heaven are instructed in his Way, his Truth, and his Life. They are equal to the angels, *the truths,* of heaven that run to and fro throughout the whole earth.

The portrayal of Elijah's translation into heaven speaks of the mind's ascent from a pseudo-spiritual to a Spiritual disposition. The adding of this higher perception is briefly portrayed in the following:

When Elijah was about to be taken up into heaven, he asked Elisha, his servant, if there was anything he wished from him. Elisha replied, "When you are taken up I would like to receive a double portion of your spirit, *as recognized in the Word's first and second reading.*"

"You ask a hard thing," said Elijah. "Nevertheless, if you see me when I am taken up, a double portion of my spirit shall be upon you."

When the time for Elijah's translation was at hand, Elisha saw the vehicle of translation that transported Elijah into heaven; and he cried, "My Father! My Father! You are the chariot of Israel, *the Spiritual translation of the Word's signs and wonders,* and the horsemen, *the truths,* thereof!"

Having recognized the Father's method of accomplishing Elijah's translation, *the translating of the visible into the invisible,* Elisha then received a double portion of Elijah's Spirit. ("He has translated us into the kingdom of his beloved Son.")

Relating to this shift in perspective, we become increasingly aware that primordial man emerged not only as the product of evolution, but was also fashioned for forthcoming involution. Made to progress in the image and likeness of all things preceding him, he was capable of receiving a double portion of God's Spirit. He was endowed with both terrestrial and celestial qualities. Not only was Creation's temporal "Tree of Knowledge" rooted in him, but Creation's eternal "Tree of Life" was also planted within his midst. To that end, God commanded his angels to have charge over him. Consequently, man's terrestrial nature witnesses to things terrestrial and his celestial nature witnesses to things celestial. Therefore, when the Son of man comes in the Father's celestial kingdom, he brings with him all the angels of the Most High, *all the Spiritual symbols of God's truth.*

We are like children who have much to learn. But to learn, we must change our ways. We must rein in our foolish excesses and put away our desire for self-justification. We must emerge from the dark void of pseudo-spiritual misinformation that presently engulfs all mankind and awaken to the Life that was prepared for us from the foundation of the world. For, until we know ourselves in the true light of our eternal heritage, our reward and our destiny will remain unfulfilled.

Epilogue

Having thoughtfully considered the material covered in *Unveiling the Mystery of Christ*, and having become knowledgeable of the truth that life's invisible content is characterized through the mirroring of countless similes, the reader should be eminently aware that by Spiritually transposing life's myriad faces, God has reconciled and made of "One Body" the continuous whole of his work. ("Whatsoever is under the whole heaven is mine.") Therein, all levels of comprehension are recognized as extensions of an eternally unified state; namely, the Collective Consciousness of the Most High. In light of this witnessing evidence, it becomes undeniably true that "the kingdom of God" and "the kingdom of heaven" are immediately available to those who would "take of the waters of Life freely."

In concert with the revelatory knowledge introduced by previous generations, *The Book of Lights* series (*Unveiling the Mystery of God, Unveiling the Mystery of Christ* and the forthcoming *Unveiling the Mystery of Life Eternal*) was prepared to shed further Spiritual light on mankind's quest for Spiritual understanding. Just as the truths introduced in these books were progressively revealed to the author, the same have been revealed to you. It has been my pleasure to share the years of Spiritual enlightenment and joy I experienced while compiling this work. In turn, I hope you will experience that same joy by sharing the truths contained on these pages with others. ("Freely have you received, freely give.") If you walk in their light, they shall serve you well. Christ's promise, "You shall know the truth, and the truth shall make you free," shall be your exceeding great reward. ("I beheld the glory and the light that was in his truth; that it was most precious, even like a Jasper stone, clear as crystal.")

GLOSSARY

This glossary is provided to aid the reader in understanding materials specifically selected for this presentation.

Adept – One whose mind is in unity with the Life-Source and is proficient in interpreting the relationship existing between the above and the below.

Cognizance – The fact of being aware or knowing; perception; knowledge.

Collective Consciousness – The Creator's collective awareness. A level of comprehension that is all-inclusive. Unity with the Source of all thought.

Continuous Whole – The aggregate of God's progressive work. The coalescing of Creation into a principle shared in common.

Covenant – A promise made by God to man, as recorded in the Bible. An agreement made by participants.

End Time – The culminating of God's revelatory work. ("It is finished.")

First Judgment – The mind's awakening to the inherent unity that relates mankind to God's work.

Illusory – Causing or caused by illusion; deceptive; unreal.

Languish – To remain unfulfilled. To lose activity and vigor.

Last Judgment – The uniting of the Spirit of God and the Spirit of man in one all-inclusive Collective Consciousness.

Light-pattern – The nonchanging principles embodied in

Creation that characterize God, Christ and Man.

Linear – The perception that all relates to time and place, that all follows the timeline continuum.

Macrocosm – Infinitely large. A universal principle. God and his Universe.

Microcosm – The infinite, *in finite*. Man as God's image and likeness. A universal simile.

Non-effect – To make void through self-exclusion or misinterpretation.

Oracle – A divine communication or revelation made known to man. The witness that signified God's presence in the Holy of Holies.

Outpictured – The transposing of Life's inherent principles into formal manifestation.

Paradise of God – The kingdom of God. The kingdom of heaven. The appearance of the Creator's work in its eternal glory.

Parallelism – In agreement; of one mind; comparable, as in the axiom, "Things equal to the same thing are equal to each other."

Passover – The mind's passage from a lower to a higher state of comprehension. ("I have greatly desired to eat this *Passover* with you.")

Pseudo-Spiritual – God is spiritual. His works are expressions of his character; they are pseudo-spiritual. All manifestation, visible and invisible, is therefore counted as pseudo-spiritual.

Quicken – To give Life to what was spiritually latent or lifeless.

Regeneration – Empowering the mind to interpret the principles embodied in pseudo-spiritual manifestation.

Resurrection – The raising of the pseudo-spiritual mind to a Spiritual level of comprehension.

Similitude – A symbol of like nature, anything that is similar to; an image and likeness; a parable; something comparable; a simile; reflective, etc.

Spiritual Translation – To remove the timeline from interpretation and view all in the eternal now. ("I AM.")

Temporal – Formed from natural elements; of an earthy nature; sensory by design; mankind's first two levels of reality.

Tenet – A principle or doctrine held as a truth.

True Light – The inherent "Light of Life" that elevates mankind into becoming intelligent beings.

Ultimate Reality – To know God; to recognize yourself in all he has made; to live in harmony with The Eternal.

Voidal – What was, is not, and yet is. Without foundation, the "bottomless pit"; to believe in error, the mind's dark misconceptions.

Way-Shower – A person who uses natural imagery to convey eternal principles; an interpreter of the Creator's work in its eternal glory.

INDEX

BOOK ORDER FORM

For additional copies of *The Book of Lights – Unveiling the Mystery of Christ*, please order via the following:

Fax Orders: 586-558-9791. Please send this form with order.

Telephone Orders: 586-573-3077

E-mail Orders: pandp_publishing@comcast.net

Postal Orders: P & P Publishing
P.O. Box 1051, Warren, Michigan 48090 U.S.A.

Please send me _____ copies at $14.95 each of
The Book of Lights – Unveiling the Mystery of Christ.

Total price of copies to be sent $_____

Add 6% sales tax (MI residents only) $_____

Add $2.00 per book, shipping/handling $_____

Total $_____

Payment: Check _____ Credit Card: VISA _____ MasterCard _____

Credit card number: _____

Cardholder's name: _____

Expiration date: _____ / _____

Cardholder's Signature: _____

---

visit us at truelightbooks.com